齊物
逍遙
2023

黃效文—— 著

# ENLIGHTENED SOJOURN

Authored and Photographed by Wong How Man

Wong How Man

*Time Magazine honored Wong How Man among their 25 Asian Heroes in 2002, calling Wong "China's most accomplished living explorer". CNN has featured his work over a dozen times, including a half-hour profile by the network's anchor. Discovery Channel has made several documentaries about his work. The Wall Street Journal has also featured him on its front page. Wong began exploring China in 1974. He is Founder/President of the China Exploration & Research Society, a non-profit organization founded in 1986 specializing in exploration, research, conservation and education in remote China and neighboring countries. Wong has led six major expeditions for the National Geographic. He successfully defined the sources of the Yangtze, Mekong, Yellow River, Salween, Irrawaddy and the Brahmaputra rivers.*

*He conducts projects in Mainland China, India, Nepal, Bhutan, Laos, Myanmar, the Philippines, and also Taiwan. In these countries or regions, he has set up centers, theme exhibits, or permanent operation bases. Wong has authored over thirty books and has received many accolades, among them an honorary doctorate from his alma mater, the University of Wisconsin at River Falls, and the Lifetime Achievement Award from Monk Hsing Yun of Taiwan. He has been invited as keynote speaker at many international functions.*

# 黃效文

《時代雜誌》在二零零二年曾選黃效文為亞洲二十五位英雄之一，稱他為「中國最有成就的在世探險家」。*CNN* 報導過黃效文的各項工作超過十二次之多，其中還包括主播 *Richard Quest* 的三十分鐘專訪。探索頻道也為他做的工作製作了好幾個紀錄片。《華爾街日報》也曾用頭版報導過他。

黃效文自一九七四年開始在中國探險。他是中國探險學會的創辦人和會長，這是個非營利組織，致力於在中國偏遠地區及鄰近國家的探險，研究，保育和教育工作。他曾經在美國《國家地理雜誌》帶領過六個重要的探險。他成功地定位的源頭包括長江，湄公河，黃河，薩爾溫江，伊洛瓦底江及雅魯藏布江。

他的學會主導的文化和自然保育項目橫跨中國和鄰近的國家，包括印度、尼泊爾、不丹、寮國、緬甸、菲律賓還有台灣。

黃效文著作的書超過三十本並獲得過許多榮譽，他的母校威斯康辛大學頒發給他名譽博士學位，星雲大師也贈與他「華人世界終身成就獎」。他也是許多國際會議裡的專題演講人。

## Preface

*I woke up quite early this morning. It was only ten past six. It drizzled a bit the night before, though here in the Jiuquan area of the Gobi Desert it seldom rains. It is rare to see dark clouds hanging over the sky. In the far-off distance, the sunrise creates a line of rainbow colors, hanging below the overcast sky.*

*The first light of dawn shines through the clouds and for two to three short minutes with its golden ray crowns the top of Jinta. Appropriately named, as jinta means golden pagoda. Perhaps due to the vegetarian diet I had the day before, I feel lighter and more at ease. This little-known temple is said to have originated during the Southern and Northern Dynasties, a period in the 4th Century. If true, it is quite possible that Fa Xian and Xuan Zang, the progenitor monks of Chinese Buddhism during the Eastern Jin and Tang Dynasties respectively, may have passed through here on their journeys to the West, albeit to India and Sri Lanka to seek the original Buddhist sutras.*

I was led here by a more contemporary monk named Fa Qi from the Nanhua Temple in Guangdong. The temple is associated with the Sixth Patriarch Master, Monk Huineng. The Jinta Temple now has three monks, which reminds me of the story of "Three Monks Fetching Water," a parable about having too many hands and so getting nothing done. However, throughout the day, I witnessed how these three monks distributed their responsibilities and worked well together in making this small temple with huge grounds a neat and orderly place.

The colorful rainbow lining and soft golden shade of the ancient pagoda become a conduit for me to roam freely with my thoughts. On our own journey west through the Qilian Mountains, we passed the Heixi Corridor of the Old Silk Road and Sunan Yugu County in Gansu Province, arriving at Qilian, a county of Qinghai Province inhabited by Tibetans and Hui.

From the grazing grounds of camel, sheep and yak, to the natural habitat of wild gazelle, red deer and marmot, having crossed two completely different geographic ecosystems and ethnically diverse regions in a short day, it feels like I am shuttling between the realm of physical excursion and that of spiritual exploration. To achieve this ideal and peaceful state, nature plays the perfect and irreplaceable role, unlike packaged tranquility and mind salvaging meditation classes offered in our modern world, often at exorbitant prices in some man-made "sanctuary."

"Think with your head and feel with your heart" - that motto has served me well for decades. For me, the analytical and intellectual functions of the left brain are a tool to serve my more subliminal senses of the right brain. Without the enjoyment of indulging in the free-spirited feeling of my right brain, the left brain's efforts are meaningless to me. Of course, everyone has his or her own aspirations, priorities and prerogatives. For some, the analytical brain and dialectics may be everything, while the the emotional parts are just appendix, abstract and impractical.

*But my "impracticals" have over the years nurtured the most valuable part of my life.  As byproduct, they even created some of the not-too-abstract undertakings that I can be proud of, such as conservation projects for nature or culture.  I hope my modest achievements can become a source of inspiration and a platform for future generations in pursuing their own dreams, surpassing the steps and journeys of my predecessors and myself.*

*With my added years and failing eyes, I find it most satisfying that life is becoming more abstract and thus also more philosophical.  This fifth book in the series of "Enlighted Sojourn" is a record that accompanies me on the road from the pandemic to the post-pandemic era, as I travel through Mainland China and its neighboring countries.  Both the obstacles and smooth parts are all inseparable parts of this journey, to be valued and enjoyed.*

*Like the four seasons as represented in Chinese by "flower in spring, breeze in summer, autumn moon and winter snow", they are all integral part and partial of a year, to be embraced and enjoy.*

# 前言

今天我早早起來，醒來時才六點過十分。前一天晚上外面下了一點毛毛雨，雖然酒泉這邊很少下雨，這時車窗外依舊是一片烏雲籠罩。在遙遠的天際線，日出形成了一道彩虹的顏色，懸掛在陰暗的天空底下。

隨即，清晨第一縷陽光穿過雲層，在不到兩到三分鐘的時間裡，金色的光照已經灑在了金塔頂上，如同給金塔加上了冠冕，讓這 "金塔" 的名字更加地恰如其分，相得益彰。可能是前一天吃了一天的素食，我感覺自己也變得輕鬆了些。這座鮮為人知的寺廟據說是起源於公元四世紀的南北朝時期。如果這是真的，那麼很可能東晉和唐朝時期，中國佛教的先祖法顯和玄奘和尚就曾經過這裡，在他們前往西方取經的路上參拜了佛塔上， 雖然他們的目的是去印度和斯裡蘭卡尋求最初的佛教典籍。

我與金塔寺的緣分始於一位來自廣東南華寺的現代僧人釋法衹法師。南華寺是佛教祖師六祖慧能的禪宗道場，被譽為嶺南禪林之冠，這次來金塔寺也是全由這位法師引薦。金塔寺一共有三個和尚，每每想到此處便使我聯想起 "三個和尚打水" 的典故。有時候人手太多，反而一事無成。然而，在金塔寺短暫停留的一天裡，我親眼目睹了這三位和尚的分工與合作，齊心協力讓這座面積龐大的寺廟維持乾淨和有序。

此刻，金塔周圍配上那柔和的金色光影，成為了我思想自由遨行的通道。我們穿越祁連山，經過古絲綢之路的河西走廊和甘肅省的肅南裕固族自治縣，到達青海省的藏族和回族少數民族聚集的祁連縣。

在短短的一天裡，我們穿越了兩個完全不同的地理生態系統和民族多樣性的地區，從駱駝、綿羊和犛牛遍佈的高原牧場，到野生羚羊、麋鹿和旱獺的自然棲息地。我感覺自己就如同穿梭在 "齊物" 與 "逍遙" 的兩個境界之間一般。為了達到這種理想的和平狀態，自然界發揮著完美和不可取代的作用。區別於我們現世中包裝過的所提供的所謂寧靜和拯救心靈的冥想課程，在一些人為製造的 "避難所" 裡付出高昂的價格。

對於我來說，齊物是左腦之思想的活動與運用，逍遙是感性右腦的享受與升華。所以我的左腦一直是為我右腦服務的工具，即如果沒有逍遙，齊物對我來 就是虛無的。當然人各有志，每個人都有自己的願景、優先和選擇。對有些人來 ，可能功能性的腦袋可以超越一切，其餘的才是抽象且不切實際的。

但這些年來，我的 "不切實際" 造就了我生命中最有價值的章節。更甚的，它創造了一些我畢生都引以為傲的不抽象的事業和成就，無論在自然還是文化保育的領域當中。我希望我微薄的努力和成就能夠成為後人追求夢想的靈感源泉和平臺，超越前人以及我自己的腳步和足跡。"用你的頭腦去思考，用你的心去感受"，這句格言在幾十年間都讓我獲益匪淺。

隨著我年齡的日漸增長和視力的衰退，我發現生活開始變得越來越抽象，且越來越哲學化，這無疑是令人欣慰的齊物與逍遙之狀態。這是我第五本以《齊物逍遙》命名的系列叢書，它伴隨著我從疫情期間走到後疫情時代，記錄著中國大陸及其周邊國家在這幾年的現狀。無論是蹣跚或坦途，這些都是這歷程中的不可分割的組成部分。風花雪月，缺一不可。

## Foreword by Thomas Pritzker

*I came to know How Man through our great friend Lodi Gyari Rinpoche. Tibetan culture is based on lineage and there was no better lineage teacher in our times than Lodi Gyari. Margot and I share with How Man a love of the Himalayas running through the Chang Tang of Tibet. How Man and I both began our visit to China in the mid-1970s; In my next life, I want to come back as How Man. Not just for his exploring the vestiges of pre-modern times, but also for the insights that come with his visits.*

*How Man comes with a provenance from the University of Wisconsin. I have known many of the great Himalayan explorers of the past 50 years and certainly count How Man amongst the most*

Pritzker on the right. Tibetogist / Pritzker（右）藏學家

prolific of those explorers.  Interestingly, many of these explores have somehow touched that same University of Wisconsin.

When you live the life of How Man, you accumulate enormous amounts of information with the attendant problem of distributing that knowledge.  While for some, this region may seem like just a small nook of mankind, having spent many, many months in the field, it is my view that the insights that come with How Man's work are some of the last and best windows onto a pre-modern swath of mankind that developed deep and constructive cultural systems and beliefs.   How Man's book documents just a portion of his amazing experiences.

# 序

我與黃效文的相識是經由我們共同的好友洛迪嘉日仁波切。西藏文化的傳承是以口傳身授、參悟體驗為主，而在我們這個時代，沒有一位上師能夠與洛迪嘉日相媲美。我的太太瑪戈特和我與效文一樣，對喜馬拉雅文化有著無限的著迷與熱愛，也因此對藏北羌塘草原的文明古國有了更深刻的一些探討和感悟。如果有輪迴，下一世我想以效文的身份再回來。這不僅僅是因為他對中國近代史諸多遺跡的探索和貢獻，還因為他對這些地方的獨特見解和詮釋。

效文來自威斯康辛大學。再過去五十年裡，我認識了許多偉大的喜馬拉雅探險家。

這其中，效文無疑是最多產的一個。而有趣的是，這些探險家中的很多人都與威斯康辛大學有著不解的緣分。

當你選擇以效文的方式生活時，你腦海中會不由地開始搜集大量的信息，同時秉承著將這些知識傳播出去的重任。雖然對一些人來說，這些地區看起來只是人類在野外度過的眾多個月的一個小角落，但我認為效文的見地與學識是未來人們了解和認識這一部分近代歷史最具建設性和系統性的窗口。這本書只是記錄了他驚人經歷的一小部分。

# 目次

當我們在深屈村

一個還不錯的開始——

# A SOMEWHAT GOOD BEGINNING AT SHAM WAT

Hong Kong – February 1, 2022

## A SOMEWHAT GOOD BEGINNING AT SHAM WAT

*My blood test report shows it all. "Cut your ice-cream, cut your starch, cut your sugar," so warned my doctor. "Unless you want to cut your legs off too," he added not so jokingly. Dr Luk was talking about my sugar count, rising between each six-month check, first to the margin and now crossing it, toward diabetes. As he was telling me, my blood pressure was rising at the same time.*

*But perhaps that index would finally go down, now that I have safely landed us into a new project at Sham Wat, a remote village with only three full-time families living by the bay at the northwestern tip of Lantau Island. Looking north toward the Pearl River Delta, one can see airplanes approaching for landing or leaving after take-off, traveling in and out of Hong Kong. For the last two years, this travel was sparse, due to the pandemic, thus contributing to my stay at home in Hong Kong, and thus forth my intake of sugar. The road bridge to Macau and Zhuhai spans across the view outside the bay.*

*Decades ago villagers were pig and vegetable farmers, but today all three families each operate a roadside-bayside snack shop, relatives turned rivals. They all sell much the same items. On the menu is bottled water, soft drinks, instant noodles, fried egg with miniature oyster, and Chinese traditional dessert soup, hot or cold. The last item is the culprit that contributed to my recent blood*

Sham Wat village from above / 俯瞰深屈村

test results.

Lien Jie, the village chief, is also proprietor of the first shop if one were hiking from Tung Chung near the airport to Tai O. The shop is now a popular stopover after three-quarters of the four-hour hike. On weekends, the flow of traffic is constant, especially during the pandemic.

As someone from outside, and in order to secure friendship for our attempt to make a comprehensive survey of the

Lien Jie & Cheong Suk at home /
蓮姐和祥叔於家裡

area, I have to visit regularly. Each time, I would order one or two bowls of a sweet dessert, be it baked sweet potato in a syrupy soup, tofu with a rich sprinkle of brown sugar, or green or red bean soup. On top of that, between autumn and spring, I would buy a large bag of tree-ripened starfruit, no doubt another contributor to my weakening kidney, as my other doctor, a traditional Chinese medical practitioner, told me.

But those tasty sacrifices have finally come to fruition, as we completed leasing of a storage shed for a pittance from Lien Jie. Within a short time, my team was able to convert this dilapidated bunker with asbestos roof into a work shed as our base to conduct multiple surveys of this isolated bay. It now has a septic tank to handle our bathroom and kitchen waste, a bunk bed, and fully operational kitchen, without changing much of its original look from the outside.

The reason I picked Sham Wat for our survey is because the bay extends for half a kilometer into the sea, very gradually. Even at high tide, one can walk out to sea for a quarter kilometer with water reaching only to the chest. Between high and low tide, the huge inter-tidal mudflat is fertile ground for all types of marine and freshwater life, with a river draining into the bay through natural mangrove forests.

The long drainage of the river into the valley hosts a large tract of farmland for the families living in the bay. Lien Jie alone has over two thousand banana plants within this stretch of land, besides growing lychee, longan and starfruit. The longan tree produces other fruit as well, as I have seen up to four pairs of beautiful Lanternflies, also known as Wax Cicada, attached to a single plant. Future seasonal surveys on insects should yield more results.

"In the 1960s, the government water department built catchment in the mid-hill and took much of our water through a tunnel to feed ShekPik Reservoir on the other side of the drainage hill. Since then, our environment has changed drastically," said Lien Jie. The river is now much smaller, dwindling to a stream during the dry winter season. But during the summer, I could drench myself lying in the stream and enjoying a cold natural spa, which I did now and then.

Since acquiring the shed, we invited partners to the area to assist in making rapid surveys for Sham Wat's natural inventory. Such work is necessary for us to understand the value of this remote bay and village, as well as to be used as baseline for the future, when more changes may occur and impact Lantau in years to come.

River, mangrove & tidal flat / 河流、紅樹林、灘塗

Dickson & team / 黃志俊和團隊

For example, the rapid vegetation survey conducted in three transects by a team led by Dr. Xoni Ma of the Outdoor Wildlife Learning Hong Kong (OWLHK), an NGO of environmental concern, produced some interesting results. The Coastal Area has a total of 22 plants recorded including 15 woody species and 7 herbaceous species. Among the 8 mangrove species reported in Hong Kong, four of them were recorded here, of which two are exotic species with invasive characteristics.

Whereas with the Village Area, due perhaps to landscaping and gardening, 47 plant species were recorded including 27 woody species and 20 herbaceous species. Of these, 25 species are exotic. One species of conservation significance, *Ceratopteris thalictroides*, was recorded near the Sham Wat Road. It is a fern species that can be found in marshes and wetland, but its population and distribution has been decreasing in recent years, and it is listed in the category II protected plants in the "List of Wild Plants under State Protection" in China.

In the Hillside Area, a total of 82 plant species were recorded including 60 woody species and 22 herbaceous species. Of these 74 are native species. Among the list, three species have conservation significance being listed in the category II protected plants. Hong Kong also lists some as "Rare and Precious Plants" in order to prevent them from being over-collected for

Lanternfly / 龍眼雞

medicinal use. Of the three, *Ceratopteristhalictroides*, is listed as "Near Threatened" in the IUCN Red List.

Though not exhaustive as a survey goes, the above sets the stage for our general knowledge of the vegetation and forest cover of Sham Wat. Simultaneously, Dickson Wong, another founder of OWLHK and a former collaborator of CERS, conducted three rapid surveys on the mudflats of Sham Wat Bay, including the small delta where the freshwater stream enters the bay. The first survey was during daytime and second one from 2 to 7 AM when the tide went out furthest. I was fortunate to join the third survey, in the wee morning hours of Chinese New Year's Eve, when the tide was at its lowest at 6 AM, receding to under 0.5 meter.

Searching on the mudflat as well as turning surface stones to examine below, the first two surveys yielded 170 species, with 73 identified so far. Those first two surveys only allowed enough time to comb the southeast section of the bay. The northwest was expected to exhibit more species, given that the pink rocky area had mangroves and weedy vegetation, and indeed our third survey met that expectation.

So far, nothing below the surface has been explored, and that would be a focus of future studies. However, our early results demonstrate a positive comparison with results from a more intensive and extensive survey done by professional experts between 2018-2021 in mangrove areas of Tung Chung near the airport. They recorded three fish species, 25 Arthropods and 23 Mollusks. Our current survey has already far surpassed their study in diversity.

For example, Hong Kong currently has eight species of fiddler crab (Uca) on record, and the Sham Wat survey yielded four of those, including a most colorful species (Uca splendida). Of mud skippers, Hong Kong hosts four types and our survey has so far turned up three of those. More than one specimen of the same horseshoe crab species was documented in the first two surveys. Given their tiny size and soft shells typical of the molting period, it is most probably a nursery ground of this important species. A while ago, CERS quietly provided seed money to a grass-roots organization for research and conservation of the horseshoe crab in Beihai of Guangxi Province in China. Now that organization has prospered, sustaining itself on its own with support from within China.

Dickson also noted an octopus stranded in one of the tidal pools, even during the daytime survey. Various shell types and shrimps are also abundant, making Sham Wat a site with high potential for future zoological and ecological education.

During the third mudflat marine survey between January 30 and 31, I invited a former young intern of CERS, a recent graduate of Oxford University with a Master in Marine Archeology, to join us. Jay Mok conducted a rapid

Fiddler Crab / 招潮蟹

Horseshoe Crab / 馬蹄蟹

Mudskipper / 彈塗魚

land survey of the old village in the bay, abandoned in the 1960s when its inhabitants moved to the present location where Lien Jie is now located. Her father, Cheong Suk, now 98, told us stories from old.

Of six houses in the past, only two remain standing, though dilapidated and in partial ruin. A quick assessment was conducted on what little remains. The next day, early morning on Chinese New Year Eve when the tide was out, Jay did a coastline-based archeological survey between 5:30 and 8:30 AM.

A zigzag pattern of survey was executed amid the changing depth of water-logged mud, since a transect grid was impossible, as each few steps would take the team sinking into deep mud. Some modern trash was identified but also old pottery, ceramic and porcelain shards. There were quite a few old fishing nets and roperies, suggesting that this might have been a decent maritime fishing hub of the Pearl River Delta.

Dickson & Jay working mudflat survey / 黃志俊和莫草泥板上調查        HM joins Dickson on survey / HM 加入黃志俊的調查

Our CERS filmmaker was also on hand to record our survey. Xavier soon fell into deep mud up to his hips, and was fortunate that two saviors were on hand to liberate him from further disgrace. As he called for help, Dante and Renato, my two Filipino helpers, rushed to pull him out of the quicksand like mud.

Just as Xavier was calling out for help, I was some two hundred meters away with Dickson, finding the biggest surprise of our entire survey. As the water receded to its lowest, barely above the sand and watermark, Dickson saw a tiny seahorse. This is a gem of a find. After photographing it, we travelled on and, another fifty meters away, we chanced upon a small horseshoe crab. I took it in my hand and felt it softly with my fingers. The shell was still soft, bending slightly to my touch.

In March of 2021, the Hong Kong government's Agriculture, Fisheries and Conservation Department (AFCD) has specially set up a "Seahorse and Adult Horseshoe Crab Sighting Report" website. It is evidence of how important such marine life is to our overall environment. I would think that a horseshoe crab nursery ground is even more important than adult sightings, thus making Sham Wat all the more special.

I however must think twice and thrice before filing a report. As with much

Seahorse / 海馬

on the internet today, once something interesting is reported online, it may bring about a stampede of "well-wishers", flooding the bay during low tide with "punch carders" to share their selfies with groupies. Perhaps our latest findings should remain a closed secret let out only to friends of relevance, and in future as ecological education site.

My mind wanders to a time in the past when there was an abundance of mud skippers, as well as mud scooters. The latter is a human-powered "vehicle" propelled by one-legged foot power, developed by ingenious seaside fisherman of Hong Kong to move around on the mudflat to collect mud skippers and oyster. How very nice an idea to revive it as a culture preservation project for students.

But for now, this is a somewhat good start in Sham Wat. As for my next blood test report, my doctor may be somewhat happy that my sugar count has miraculously dropped down. No more sweet dessert is needed now that Lien Jie has become a good friend. As with our new project, despite being on the murky mudflat, it has gained some traction.

Mud scooter at mud flat across Shenzhen / 泥板車在灘塗上橫跨深圳

# 一個還不錯的開始——當我們在深屈村

我的血液報告，一目了然。「砍掉你的冰淇淋、澱粉和糖。」醫生的警告還沒結束，「除非你想砍掉兩隻腳！」聽起來不妙，似乎不像開玩笑。陸醫生說的是我的糖份超標問題——在每半年的檢查之間，我的血糖值不斷攀升，先是在危險邊界浮動，現在則衝破紅線，離糖尿病不遠矣。醫生還提醒我，我的血壓也同時升高了。

不過，也許這些指數最終都會緩緩降下，不管怎樣，反正我們現在已安全抵達新計畫的終點站——大嶼山西北海灣旁的深屈村——一個只有三戶人家長年定居島上的偏遠村莊。朝北方望向珠江三角州，一抬頭便能瞥見正在降落或衝破雲霄的飛機身影，在香港機場起降出入。前方通往澳門與珠海的路橋，就在橫跨海灣之外的景色中。過去兩年因疫情爆發，頻繁的跨國旅行近乎不可能，或許因為被迫待在香港家裡足不出戶，才搞得我血糖指數不斷飆高……。

數十年前，這裡的村民都是養豬戶與菜農，但今天這三戶家庭都各自經營起路邊小吃店，親戚家族頓時成了商業競爭對手。他們賣的東西大同小異，菜單上選項不多，就是瓶裝水、汽水、即食麵、小牡蠣炒蛋、中式傳統冷熱甜湯。顯然，最後一項飲品是我血液測試結果不佳的罪魁禍首。

如果從機場附近的東涌徒步往大澳走來，一段四小時的健行走到
四分之三時，第一個停靠站，就是村長蓮姐的餐飲店。這家小店
已成為最受旅人歡迎的休憩站，尤其週末，人潮川流不息；即使
疫情期間，往來群眾也有增無減。

身為外來旅客，如果想要對當地進行全面性的研究與調查，我們
有必要與居民保有一定程度的交情，也因此，我定期前往村長的
餐飲店報到。每一次總免不了要消費一兩份點心，無論是糖水烤
地瓜、灑上滿滿黃糖的豆花、紅豆沙或綠豆沙等，滿滿的甜蜜。
除此以外，若遇春秋嬗遞之際，我還會買一大袋樹上熟的楊桃，
難怪我的另一位傳統中醫師也告誡我要注意腎功能的問題，看
來，這水果恐怕也是另一個禍源了。

不過，這些「美味的代價」最終開花結果，讓我們如願以不多的
費用從村長蓮姐那裡租下一間儲藏室。我的團隊在很短的時間
內，把這個石綿屋瓦的破舊倉房，改造成工作室，作為研究基地，
方便我們對這孤立海灣進行觀測與調查。改頭換面的工作室，設
了個化糞池，可以處理廁所與廚房廢棄物，臥室有張上下床鋪，
還有設備完善的廚房；但從外觀上看來倒是和原來的倉房沒太大
差別。

把深屈村作為研究目標的原因，其實很單純：因為海灣以非常平

Map of Sham Wat Bay / 深屈灣地圖
Bay with bridge & plane landing /
海灣、橋和飛機降落

緩的坡度延伸了半公里才到深海裡。即使漲潮時，你還可以肆無忌憚向大海方向慢走長達四分之一公里，潮水也只衝到你的胸部。潮水漲退之間，巨大的潮間泥灘成了各種海洋與淡水生物的沃土，此外，還有一條穿越天然紅樹林、排入海灣的河流。

這條流經山谷的排水溝，細水長流，為居住在海灣的家庭孕育了大片農田。光是村長蓮姐一戶人家，就種了兩千多棵香蕉樹，另外還有荔枝、龍眼與楊桃等果樹。其中的龍眼樹，結實纍纍，我還曾看過四對美麗的斑點燈籠蠅——也稱為蠟蟬 (Wax Cicada)，附著於一株龍眼樹上。未來如果著眼於昆蟲的季節性調查，成果必然可期。

蓮姐說：「六〇年代期間，政府的水務局在半山腰蓋了集水區，透過一條地下水道把我們大部分的水引到另一側的排水山區，注入『石壁水塘』。」因此，今天我們看到的這條河流窄小得多，尤其在乾燥的冬季時，水流越來越少，從河流瘦身成小溪。但一到夏天，我經常恣意躺在溪流裡淋雨，雨水像涼冷的天然水療，沁人心脾。

Outside shed / 倉房外　　　　　　　　　　　　　　　　Inside shed / 倉房內

打造好團隊的工作室，有了個落腳處，我們開始邀請合作夥伴前來，為深屈村的天然資源進行初步調查。這些研究工作有助於我們了解這個偏遠海灣與村莊的價值，同時把調查結果建檔入庫，作為未來進一步研究大嶼山任何變化與衝擊的基礎資訊。

舉個例子，以關懷環境教育與生態保育的非政府組織「香港戶外生態教育協會」(OWLHK)，在馬昀祺 (Xoni Ma) 博士的指導下，已完成當地三個橫斷面的植被調查，也取得一些可觀的數據與成果——沿海地區共紀錄了二十二種植物，其中包括十五種木本植物與七種草本植物。香港有紀錄在冊的八種紅樹林物種中，單是這地方便占了四種，其中兩種則是具威脅性的外來種。

以鄉村區域來說，或許因景觀與園藝因素，這裡紀錄了四十七種植物，包括二十七種木本植物與二十種草本植物；其中二十五種為外來種。我們另外在深屈路附近紀錄到一個獨特的保育類物種：水蕨 (Ceratopteris thalictroides)。這些生長於沼澤地與濕地的蕨類植物，近年來無論數量與分布都不斷減少，在中國的《國家重點保護野生動物名錄》裡，水蕨被列為二級保護類級別。

至於山坡區的紀錄就更豐富多元了，總計有八十二種植物，包括六十種木本植物與二十二種草本植物，其中七十四種為原生種。根據保護名錄，其中三種被列入第二類級的保護植物。香港也將其中一些植物列為「稀有及珍貴植物」，以防被過度採集當藥用。在這三種植物中，根據「國際自然保護聯盟瀕危物種紅色名錄」(IUCN Red List)，水蕨屬於「近危」的保護級別。

縱使這些調查不算太詳盡，但整體而言，初步的觀察紀錄所得的結果，已足以讓我們對深屈村的植被與森林覆蓋地建立一定程度的基礎知識與概覽。身兼「中國探險學會」的前合作夥伴與「香港戶外生態教育協會」的另一位創辦人黃志俊 (Dickson Wong)，幾乎同一時候也針對深屈灣的泥灘進行三

Xoni & Janice / 馬昀祺和勞丕禮
Ceratopteris thalictroides / 水蕨

次初步調查，包括流進海灣的淡水溪流匯聚成的小小三角洲。第一次調查在白天執行，第二次則選定於潮水退得最遠的凌晨兩點至上午七點之間。我很榮幸得以參加第三次調查，就在農曆新年前夕，我們從凌晨一直等到潮水最低的清晨六點，當時潮水已退到零點五公尺以下。

在泥灘上搜尋物種時，需要把一顆顆石頭翻面檢查；前兩次的調查時間有限，而且範圍也僅限於海灣東南方，但成果不少，到目前為止，我們已紀錄了一百七十個物種，其中七十三種已被確認。由於粉紅岩石區一帶有紅樹林與雜草植被，估計西北區域會有更多外來種；第三次調查結果一如所料，完成預期計畫。

我們至今仍未找到任何地底下的物種，這將成為我們未來研究的重點目標。不過，如果和二〇一八至二〇二一年期間由專家學者在機場附近的東涌紅樹林區所進行的調查結果相比，我們這一次的初步研究，收穫豐碩，也令人欣慰。當時的調查比較著重深度與廣度，他們紀錄了三種魚類、二十五種節肢動物與二十三種軟體動物；但我們這一次的調查成果在生物多樣性方面，已遠遠超過這些物種。

譬如，香港目前有紀錄的招潮蟹 (Uca) 總計八種不同類別，深屈村的調查結果就發現了其中四種，包括色彩最繽紛、俗稱紅腳仙

的麗彩招潮蟹 *(Uca splendida)*。以泥鰍來說，香港紀錄在案的四種類中，我們已在當地找到其中三種，而在前兩次調查中，我們紀錄下的馬蹄蟹——鱟 *(horseshoe crab)*，至少超過一種。體小而軟殼的鱟，尤其在蛻殼期間，這些地區很可能成為牠們繁殖與生長的理想居所。不久前，「中國探險學會」曾私下提供種子資金給一家位於廣西省北海的基層組織，如今，這個以研究與保育鱟為目標的基層組織成長得茁壯，並在國內的支持下，已能有自給自足的經費。

有一次在白天進行的調查中，黃志俊甚至注意到擱淺在其中一個潮汐池的章魚。顯然，這一帶的貝殼與蝦類豐富多元，從未來動物學與生態學的教育環境來說，深屈村無疑是個潛力十足的場域。

在一月三十與三十一日之間執行第三次泥灘海洋調查時，我邀請了之前曾在「中國探險學會」實習的莫草 *(Jay Mok)*——剛從牛津大學海洋考古研究碩士畢業的年輕學者——加入我們的團隊。莫草對一個六〇年代被遺棄的海灣舊村落進行初步的土地調查時，早期的村民早已移居到蓮姐目前的村莊。蓮姐的父親，今年高齡九十八歲的祥叔，對我們娓娓道來一段久遠的老故事。

當年的六戶家庭已人去樓空，僅存的兩間空房子雖然部分結構還在，但實際上已破敗不堪，形同廢墟，不過，我們還是對殘缺不全的老房舍進行初步評估。隔天，農曆新年前一天，大約清晨五點半到八點半之間，潮水退盡後，莫草執行了以海岸線為基準的考古調查。

要在變幻莫測的積水泥灘上進行調查，選項不多，只能採取鋸齒模式，曲折前進；因為每走幾步就會深陷泥淖，所以，我們只能放棄橫斷的網狀調查模式。除了發現舊時代的陶器、陶瓷與殘瓦碎片，卻也發現一些「現代」的新垃圾。除此之外，我們也發掘不少舊式漁網與繩索，這些古物似乎暗示，當地可能是珠江三角州曾經繁榮一時的海上漁業中心。

我們的「中國探險學會」電影製作人李伯達 (Xavier) 也在現場紀錄所有調查工作。拍攝過程中，伯達一不留神便急速陷落深達臀部的泥漿裡，他立刻大聲呼救，所幸身邊兩位菲律賓助理丹提 (Dante) 與雷納多 (Renato) 及時出手，把他從急流泥沙中拉拔起來，否則，狼狽後果不堪設想。

就在伯達求救的同一時間，我和黃志俊在兩百公尺外進行調查，那一次的工作成果大有斬獲——引來我們整個調查中最大的驚喜！當潮水退到最低最遠時，只剩一些海水在沙地與水位標誌上，志俊發現了一隻小海馬。就像發現珍稀寶石般，令人欣喜若狂。拍完照後，我們繼續前進，走了大約五十公尺，不經意一瞥，竟發現一隻小小鱟。我把這隻也被稱為馬蹄蟹的小生物握在手上，手腹輕撫。馬蹄蟹的殼仍是軟的，在我的觸摸下微微蜷曲。

二〇二一年三月，港府的「漁農自然護理署」(AFCD) 特別設立了《香港水域海馬及成年海鱟報告》(Seahorse and Adult Horseshoe Crab Sighting Report) 網站。由此可見，這些海洋生

Jay & Dickson early morning / 莫草和黃志俊於清晨

物對我們的整體外在生態環境，舉足輕重。我認為，海鱟的育苗之地比成年的棲息地更重要，也因此，深屈村更顯意義不凡。

然而，在撰寫報告之前，我千頭萬緒，深感自己必須三思而行。一如今天網路上的資訊，一旦什麼奇聞軼事幾經報導轉發而登上熱搜，我已可以預見，一定引來一群「善心的環保人士」蜂擁至海灣，守候退潮時猛「打卡」再和群組網友分享自拍照。我想，或許我們應該把這些最新的發現，當成封閉式的秘密，只分享給相關的朋友群體，並作為未來生態教育的網站。

我的思緒紛飛，想起那遍地泥鰍與泥板車的年代。其實，泥滑板是單腳後推的人力「交通工具」，由中國沿海的漁民研發開創的載具，聰明的漁民藉此工具在泥灘上移動，方便採集泥鰍與牡蠣。如果能把這些舊工具，復原成現代學生的文化保存物而代代相傳，該有多好啊！

但以目前的狀況來說，能在深屈村有這些成果與收穫，已是個不錯的起點。至於我下一次的血液報告，也許我的醫生會因為我的血糖指數奇蹟式下降而為我開心。我現在已不需要再吃甜點了，因為蓮姐已成為我的的好朋友了。一如我們的新計畫，儘管總是在坑窪泥濘裡工作，但步步難行最終依舊能找到牽引前進的力量。

Xavier's savior / 李伯達的救主
Horseshoe crab / 馬蹄蟹
Mudflat survey results / 灘塗調研成果

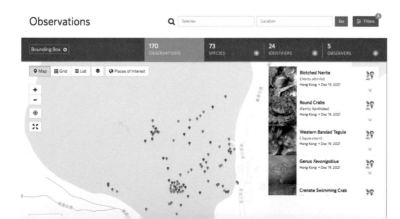

醒
一
醒

# WAKE UP CALL

Sham Wat, Lantau, Hong Kong – March 5, 2022

## *WAKE UP CALL*

*This is not your hotel wake up call.  This is nothing like your mobile phone alarm.  This is a wake up call from long before there were hotels and phones.  It is something that the natural world has abided by for centuries, if not millennia.*

*It comes as clouds collide and begins each year with the call of spring through thunder.  "Jing Zhe" is the third of twenty-four increments of the Chinese annual solar calendar; something farmers follow, as the sun is far more important to agriculture than the moon of a lunar-based calendar.  Every two weeks, a new climate segment unfolds, corresponding to weather changes, which in turn dictate the time for planting, growing or harvesting crops, depending on what crop a farmer is involved with.*

*Even as Chinese characters go, Jing Zhe is full of meaning. "Jing" means "waking," not in a mild sense, but more like "shocked" or even "panicked" into arising.  "Zhe" relates to insects, and as such, refers to insects and their larvae hibernating underground.  So "Jing Zhe" signifies that insects are shocked into arising by a rather brutal wake-up call; the first sound of thunder. As the sun's angle hits 345° according to the Chinese solar calendar and calculations of orbital dynamics, "Jing Zhe" falls on either March 5 or 6.  In 2022, it actually starts at 22:44, an hour or so before midnight on March 5.  It was a few minutes in the count down to this moment when I started writing.*

*Earlier today, we were having a foggy day which gradually cleared up to an almost spotless clear sky. By evening with a new moon, stars were showing in the partially lit sky of Hong Kong. It does not seem like the clouds will come any time soon to call up thunder. But we shall see in the morning.*

*As the insects are supposed to wake up and come to the surface, we chose today, March 5, to conduct our insect survey at the new CERS project site of Sham Wat on Lantau Island. We recently finished rapid surveys of the area's vegetation and of marine life on the tidal flat, as well as a basic archaeological report.*

*Though the new strain of Omicron is creating havoc in Hong Kong, with tens of thousands infected daily, our small team headed out to Sham Wat, one of the remotest villages of Hong Kong, and probably one of the safest during the pandemic's rage. With only three active families living there, the CERS Field Shed, our newest field base, can be considered the fourth household in this isolated village.*

*Bond and Janice are two of three co-founders of Outdoor Wildlife Learning (OWLHK), a five-year old local NGO and partner with CERS on the current survey. Natalie, CERS filmmaker, is also on hand to document any new findings. My Filipino team of brothers Dante and Renato brought tools to make final touches to our field shed, whereas Berry and Randy perform logistic support duties, restocking our tiny pantry and preparing lunch and a snack. I, as always, loiter around as the curious observer.*

*Around an hour after Bond and Janice started off upstream from a river that drains into the bay, I follow suit, allowing them ample time to work quietly before this inquisitive ex-journalist enters the bush. Upon our rendezvous, Bond told me that the mayflies are out early and can be seen already, not in May, but in March. Yes,*

Colorful moth / 色彩鮮明的蛾

this winter has been exceptionally warm.  Even my favorite Kapok Trees by the roadside are all bearing flowers already.

On both sides of this river, now trickling like a small stream before rainy season arrives, are large tracts of banana palms.  There are also lychees and long-an trees around.  The Long-an Lanternfly, a type of wax cicada called "Long-an Chicken" by local Chinese, are most colorful and can easily be seen attached to the many long-an trees.  Within one morning, I have seen and photographed over half a dozen specimens.  Meanwhile, I also captured a beautiful Paris Peacock butterfly.

Lunch, veggie pizza and sandwiches, are served as everyone takes a break around 1pm.  Our Filipino contingent opts for a rice dish they had prepared ahead; without rice, they consider no meal has been taken.

After lunch, I see a jumping spider hopping onto the leftover pizza on our plate, and on the side of the corrugated wall of our shed, a colorful moth, Eressa confinis, with an orange banded body.  The survey team swings to the north side of the bay where the old Sham Wat Village used to be, before 1962, when a fierce typhoon hit Hong Kong and devastated the houses, forcing a move to the current newer village across the bay.

Janice & Bond / 勞丕禮和沈鼎榮

At 3pm, Bond and Janice come back to announce the biggest surprise of the day, sighting of a Fluffy Tit Butterfly, *Zeltus amasa maximinianus*. This butterfly was first discovered in Hong Kong only last year, at Tai O Village an hour away from Sham Wat. Prior to that sighting, it has never been known to exist in Hong Kong, being a species from a much warmer region far to the South.

Perhaps climate change has brought tropical species closer and closer to our subtropical region, including many species formerly unknown to Hong Kong. Seeing this orange-yellow spotted butterfly with two long protruding tails so early in the spring suggests that its larva has survived the local winter, a most appropriate wakening on today's "Jing Zhe".

For Hong Kong as well as some towns in Guangdong province, "Jing Zhe" is also a day when a traditional ritual is performed. At temples and shrines around the city, elderly ladies offer service in "Pounding the Little Person". It is believed that any misfortune and bad luck befalling someone is due to the spells or misdeeds of one's enemy, the so-called "Little Person".

So, on this day, one can bring the name and identity of such an enemy to these elderly ladies who have special connections to deities above or below our earth. Upon paying a nominal fee, the name of the person in question will be written on a secretive slip of paper, which will then be put down on an altar and fiercely and repeatedly pounded with an old slipper or shoe, accompanied by special chants while incense and paper offerings are burnt.

This act is supposed to wake up and shock the enemy so that he or she would stop performing misdeeds. It is not unusual to see young women, and even occasionally men, lining up to beat up their spouse or lover, or even rivals in business, or enemies of their loved ones. I have even seen Filipino domestic helpers adopting and paying for this Chinese practice, which I hope is not for revenge through a curse on their employers.

But this year, like so many activities, this practice is momentarily banned, due to the pandemic that has restricted gathering of people. I have observed the melee during previous "Jing Zhe." On any regular year, one popular site in Causeway Bay would be bustling, crowded with hate-wishers lining up to have a chance to perform an awakening ritual. This year, all will be quiet.

Perhaps more important of an awakening is not just for the insects, nor as revenge for those who have been wronged or bewitched. We humans must wake up to the calls of nature, like the sightings of the Fluffy Tit Butterfly and the early mayflies. Global warming and climate change are problems incurred by our past actions, and must be solved also with our own initiatives. This awakening will allow us to leave behind a better world for our future generation to live in.

Fluffy Ti Butterfly / 珍灰蝶

# 醒一醒

這不是飯店叫醒你的服務電話，也完全不是你手機裡傳來的鬧鐘響鈴。這種喚醒你的方式，比飯店和手機的存在，更久遠、更亙古。那是自然界遵行了好幾個世紀、甚至數千年來的節氣。

它在雲層的碰撞間出現，每一年當天氣回暖時，透過春雷初鳴，把蟄伏的萬物，從冬眠中驚醒。「驚蟄」是中國年曆的太陽曆中，二十四節氣的第三節；農民遵循這節氣，因為太陽對農作耕耘的重要性，遠超乎農曆的月亮。每兩個星期，一個全新的天候節氣啟動，與氣象變化相呼應，再回過頭來決定何時播種、生長或收穫的時間，當然，其中還得以農民選擇何種作物為判斷。

如果單從漢字來一窺「驚蟄」之原意，其實已昭然若揭。「驚」有驚醒的意思，毫不溫和委婉，而是傾向「驚嚇」或甚至「驚慌叫醒你」的態勢。從字面來看，「蟄」顯然與昆蟲有關，因此，指的就是躲在地下冬眠的昆蟲與其幼蟲。因此，「驚蟄」意味著以一種猛烈粗暴的第一聲轟轟春雷，石破天驚，叫醒昆蟲。根據中國太陽曆與軌道動力學的計算，當太陽轉到三百四十度時，「驚蟄」就落在三月五日或六日。以二〇二二年為例，精準的驚蟄節氣，從夜間十點四十四分開始，亦即三月五日的午夜前一兩個小時。就在我伏案書寫的此時此刻，倒數計時還有幾分鐘，便是驚蟄之始。

今天稍早，天空霧濛濛一片，隨後便撥雲見日，晴空萬里。入夜前，一輪明月高掛，香港的部份天空還能見到星星。看來，雲層還不會轉瞬招來響雷。但隔日上午應該就會聞雷而驚醒了。

於是，我們就選定今天，三月五日，在昆蟲驚醒、出沒、現蹤跡的大好日子，在「中國探險學會」的新計畫區——大嶼山的深屈村進行田野調查。我們最近已針對這區域的植被與潮灘上的海洋生物，完成初步調查，包括一份概略性的考古基本報告。

儘管新冠病毒在香港肆虐而造成巨大破壞與傷亡，每天有數萬人感染與隔離，但我們的研究小團隊依舊不改行程，前往香港其中一個最偏遠的深屈村工作，或許也是病毒大流行期間最安全的村莊之一吧。村內目前只有三戶常住的人家，而「中國探險學會」打造的工作室，是我們最新的田野基地，勉強可以湊合成這個偏遠村莊的第四戶人家吧。

成立僅五年的非政府組織「香港戶外生態教育協會」(OWLHK) 的其中兩位創辦人沈鼎榮 (Bond) 與勞丕禮 (Janice)，夥同「中國探險學會」共同參與這項調查。我們的電影製作人 Natalie 也在現場紀錄我們的任何新發現。我的菲律賓助理兄弟丹提 (Dante) 與雷納多 (Renato) 把工具備好，進行田野基地工作室的最後修整；而 Berry 與 Randy 則負責後勤支援，為我們小小的儲藏室補給食物，準備午餐與點心。至於我，一如以往，當個稱職的好奇觀察者，在附近周遊閒晃。

鼎榮與丕禮已從匯入海灣的一條河流上游處出發，大約一小時後，我也跟了上去，讓他們有充裕的時間安靜工作，免得被我這個老愛尋蹤覓跡的前記者，深入水木叢裡打擾他們。當我們會合後，鼎榮告訴我，原來五月才會出現的蜉蝣，竟已迫不及待提早到三月出現。確實，今年暖冬呢。我最愛的木棉花樹也已熱鬧登場，春暖花開。

Lanternfly / 龍眼雞

河流兩旁種植大片香蕉樹，雨季之前，涓涓汩流的河流宛若一條小溪。除了香蕉樹，周遭還種了荔枝與龍眼樹。龍眼樹上的燈籠蠅，當地華人稱之為「龍眼雞」，是一種色澤豔麗的蠟蟬，一眼望去，好多龍眼樹上都可輕易看到牠們的身影。光是一個上午，我便已拍下六種以上的標本。我還同時意外發現了迷人的巴黎孔雀蝴蝶。

下午一點，大家午休，我們的午餐是素食披薩與三明治。我們的菲律賓兄弟代表隊吃的是他們預先準備好的米飯，對他們來說，沒有米飯等於沒吃過正餐。

午餐後，我瞥見一隻活蹦亂跳的蜘蛛一躍跳到盤子裡，停留在吃剩的披薩上，一轉頭，只見一隻身軀橙黃帶狀、五彩繽紛的斑腹鹿蛾 (Eressa confinis)，飛到工作室的波紋牆一側，靜止不動。坐在這兒抬頭轉眼，所見都是蟲。飽餐一頓後，調查團隊繼續工作，大夥兒齊聚到海灣北方的老舊深屈村。一九六二年前，香港曾經遭受一次猛烈颱風的襲擊，當年的天災也把這些房屋摧毀得面目全非，迫使當地居民不得不遷移到現在的新村。

午後三點，鼎榮與丕禮結束工作返回，同時帶回當天最大的大好消息——他們看到一隻罕見的珍灰蝶 (Zeltus amasa maximinianus)！這類蝴蝶是去年才在香港首次被發現，發現地是離深屈村一小時路程的大澳村。在此之前，這類物種向來只在較溫暖的南方區域出現，從未在香港現蹤跡。或許氣候變遷，縮短了熱帶物種與亞熱帶區之間的距離，這些嬌客離我們越來越近了，其中還包括許多過去在香港地區不為人知的物種，近期也紛紛出現。能在初春時分便已看到夾著兩條長尾巴的橙黃斑蝶，表明牠的幼蟲已在當地熬過漫漫寒冬——如此呼喚與甦醒，最適切於詮釋今天的「驚蟄」了。

以香港與廣東省的一些城鎮來說，「驚蟄」還是個充滿傳統禮儀的日子。驚蟄時節，城市周遭的寺廟與神社裡外，人聲鼎沸，年長女士為民「除害」，施行「打小人」儀式與服務。相信傳統習俗的人認為，所有不幸和厄運臨頭，都要歸咎於個人仇敵的詛咒與罪行，而這些仇敵就是所謂的「小人」。

因此，一到「驚蟄」這天，信眾把仇敵「小人」的名字與身分報上，告知這些上達天庭、下達地府的通靈老太太。支付了一筆象徵性的費用後，把「小人」的大名寫在一張神秘紙條上，再把紙條放置祭壇，取一舊拖鞋或鞋子，一邊反覆用力敲打紙條，一邊念念有詞，同時還要點香燒金紙，祭拜一番，確保使命達成。

Sham Wat field shed / 深屈村倉房　　　　　　　Dante & Renato / 丹堤和雷納多

此舉不外乎把敵人叫醒再警告驚嚇之，好讓小人不再得逞，停止為非作歹。我們經常也看到年輕女子甚至偶爾包括年輕男性排隊進場，準備把自己的不如意配偶、愛人、生意上的對手或不共戴天的親人仇敵，請通靈阿婆狠狠教訓，「痛打一頓」。我也曾看過菲律賓籍的家庭幫傭入境隨俗，也以中國傳統方式來「花錢消災」，我暗地裡希望她們不是要對雇主施展復仇計畫。

可惜的是，今年的驚蟄打小人儀式一如其他活動，因疫情爆發而嚴禁群聚、暫停舉辦。我倒是曾在之前的「驚蟄」中觀察過這些人群湧動的混亂場面。在狀況正常的任何年節裡，銅鑼灣的其中一個熱門地點最熱鬧，整條街擠滿了「復仇者」，排隊守候，勢必要行禮如儀，掌握「驚蟄」先機。而今年，喧鬧場面不復見，一片沉寂。

或許，更重要的召喚與覺醒，不是只為昆蟲，也不是專為被錯待或被蠱惑的人視為報復好時機。生而為人，我們都必須對大自然的喚醒有所覺知，一如瞥見珍灰蝶與提早現身的蜉蝣，或許都是對我們的警示。全球暖化與氣候變遷的問題，是我們過去種下的禍根，理當也要由我們主動解決。這樣的覺醒，促請我們要為下一代保留一個更美好的世界，讓他們在此安身立命。

Pounding Little Person / 打小人

河川探源——
額爾濟斯河

# HEADWATERS OF THE IRTYSH

Irtysh River, Xinjiang – May 1, 2022

# HEADWATERS OF THE IRTYSH
## Only river of China flowing into the Arctic Ocean

*I've been obsessed with rivers of Asia for decades, with exploration over the years of multiple river sources that originate in China. Usually, they empty into the East China Sea, like the Yangtze and the Yellow River, or pass through South or Southeast Asia, like the Mekong, Salween, Irrawaddy and Brahmaputra, all of which we have reached and defined their sources.*

*Finally, I have a chance to visit the Irtysh, headwaters of the Ob International River System, a system that starts from the Altay Mountains, flowing through northern Xinjiang of China, then into Kazakhstan and ultimately through Siberian Russia before it empties into the Kara Sea of the Arctic Ocean. That makes it, at 5410 kilometers, the seventh longest river system in the world, and it is also the seventh headwaters of a major river that I have explored.*

*Locally, near its source, the Irtysh River is also known to the Kazaks as Kuyierterhe, or Yaerqixihe. Traveling through various ethnic communities and countries, it changes names more frequently than the seasons. From source to mouth, the water flows on a journey of 5,410 km. My journey has taken me nearly as far, from the Pearl River Delta in China's southeast, over a period of three weeks of driving, to the furthermost northwest corner of China. Needless to say, the first three* weeks hotel quarantine during the pandemic felt like it added months to the journey. But the joy of reaching such a remote and pristine area made the time spent well worth it.

With connection and help from Chu Wen, our first CERS Young Scholar and a wildlife biologist PhD candidate and animal rescue specialist, we managed to enter with our entire caravan into the wonderland of Koktokay. Normally the area, once a glaciated valley now gazetted as Keketuohai UNESCO Global Geopark, is forbidden to vehicles except for those of the local Kazak herders who traditionally reside here during the summer months.

Headwater of Irtysh / 額爾濟斯河源頭

The name Keketuohai suggests a lake or sea, but actually the Kazak name, Koktokay, means turquoise green forest. It has also been called China's Yosemite. It is a place of huge granite boulders and rock massifs, some rising to hundreds of meters in the shape of domes or with sheer cliffs. Legend has it that there are 108 peaks, and that a visit to see Sacred Bell Dome, rising 385 meters from the valley floor, resembling a somewhat lower El Capitan, will ensure a safe and sound life. Embedded between the peaks is the Irtysh River, meandering through alpine meadows and valleys in a deep canyon. Such is part of the basis for setting up a Geological Park with exhibits about these glacier-formed mountains and valleys.

In 2010, the government submitted a proposal to UNESCO seeking to list the area as a World Heritage Site, citing the region's special geological and glacial formations with headwaters of an important river with great biodiversity. However, it has yet to be recognized formally. While the area of Koktokay now seeks more international recognition, from some seventy years ago until the late 1990s, the area was considered a top military secret for the country.

Sacred Bell Dome / 神鐘山

Geological features / 地質特徵

Close-up of features / 特徵近照

The Koktokay Number 3 Mine was once reported to be the largest open pit pegmatite mine in the world, providing ore with up to 86 types of minerals among the some 140 known to the world, including some of the most rare, radioactive and valuable ones. The list cited takes up more than half of the Periodic Table. In the 1960s, ores mined here provided enough value to cover almost half of the debt payment China owed to the Soviet Union. It was also crucial in providing the core material for China's nuclear weapons and aerospace programs. Such programs were essential and used as strategic deterrent to threat and blackmail by other powers in maintaining China's sovereign rights.

Mine quarry / 礦場

With a depth of 200 meters and a 2.5 km footpath snaking down its steep sides, some people have called it the Mecca for geologists. Today, the site is open to tourists for visit. We made a stop there, as well as visit the Geological Exhibition Hall nearby, once the home of the Soviet-Sino Workers Association when both countries have their scientists, mining experts and miners working together during the honeymoon period of the early PRC.

The terrain and physical features of the valley remind me of earlier days I spent in Yosemite and the High Sierras in the US, where I camped at times even during winter. Here as there, the snow from last winter still covers the snow-capped mountains on higher grounds. It also somewhat resembles my home in Millard Canyon inside the Angeles National Forest in California where I lived in a log house for ten years.

Here is traditional grazing ground for the Kazak nomads during the summer, before they move camp upcountry with their livestock. But spring is still around the corner, and we could see Kazaks herding their livestock, including sheep, cows and even a few camels, up the valley to higher pasture. The new season is calling, and the land is about to turn from gray and brown to yellow and green. Not only are the Kazak nomads migrating, migrating birds also use the Irtysh River as a temporary stopover or as home for their summer nesting.

Tiny yellow flowers are popping up on the green field that is like a new carpet laid before us. The birch and poplar forest are showing red and green buds on treetops, among taller evergreens, fir and pine, in the riparian forest. To the north, on the more shaded side of the hills, thick snow from the last season can still be seen along the road. Along the banks of the Irtysh where we set camp, the snow has not fully melted - a perfect natural freezer to keep our wine and beer chilled.

The army border sentry before Mongolia is only a short distance away, barely a couple of kilometers up the road, with the international border maybe forty kilometers to our northeast as the crow flies. In the afternoon of our arrival, Chu Wen cleverly turned around within sight of the outpost so our small caravan will not be questioned. We chose an ideal spot by the river as our campground, saving excursion beyond the checkpoint for the last day of our stay. This would allow us to explore the safer buffer zone and interview isolated Kazak communities, as well as collect much-needed cultural

Tall snow bank / 高聳的雪堆

artifacts for the new Xinjiang Pavilion back at our home base in Zhongdian, a.k.a. Shangri-la.

On the second day, while our team went to a nearby Kazak community to collect artifacts and conduct interviews, I took the opportunity to hike up a ridge towards a granite dome. Several eagles circled overhead looking for prey - a pika, vole or marmot coming out from a long winter of hibernation to catch the sun. Arriving at the ridge after about an hour, the panoramic view of the valley beyond, as well as looking down at our camp, was most spectacular.

Perhaps the most exceptional feature among the dome-like granite, sometimes snow-capped, was at the entrance gate into the park. Here on the west side of the dome was a fascinating comb-like carving, like a beehive, but obviously a remnant footprint of the last glacier age. This feature would repeat itself further upriver as we reached the famous Sacred Bell Dome. Indeed, nature's sculpture again demonstrates that man-made "art" pieces are no match. Nonetheless, our highly commercial

Kazak yurts / 哈薩克帳篷                    View from ridge / 從山嶺的景觀

market cannot sell nature to hang in a home, thus must create something to induce sale and profit. Photo images, however, can hardly capture the full grandiose spectacle.

Beyond the Sacred Bell, we went eight kilometers upstream to where the road ends, with barbed wire and a sign warning anyone from going beyond. At this spot, I am 34 kilometers from the ridge, and perhaps 600 meters in elevation below the watershed where the source begins.

Strolling so close to the source of another great river, I feel both proud and humbled to occupy my tiny existential speck among nature. However, I can understand that to those living their entire lives in urban cities with egocentric self-identity, my thoughts may seem irrelevant and silly. Indeed, when I live for any length of time in the city, even my self-esteem and ego tend to be inflated as well. Here with nature is a reality check and my best remedy. I can imagine that our humbled Earth, looking up at constellations and galaxies, may likewise feel some humility, relatively that is.

Sitting by the bank of the Irtysh and bathing myself in the afternoon sun, another thought comes up momentarily. I need to do my laundry, after being on the road for weeks. However, on second thought, I decide that the idea is out of sync with such natural beauty, sending my filth to probably

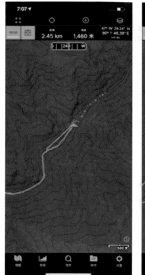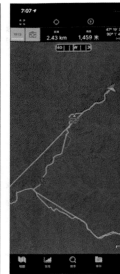

Route map to watershed /
到分水嶺的路徑地圖

Headstream with waterfall / 源頭水流和瀑布

the purest of oceans on earth, the Kara Sea of the Arctic Ocean. Organic as my dirt may be, it is not at all romantic. I wisely give up the thought and continue to soak up the sun as well as the scenery.

By evening, the sun has painted the dome above a golden yellow. It is 9 pm before the last ray fades away. Xinjiang should be three hours in time-zone away from Beijing but, for matters of official convenience, maintains the same clock time as the capital. For me however, once in the field the hours, days, weeks, even months, are no longer relevant, and lost in the space of time. Even so, the night air chills quickly as stars fill the sky as canopy, with a new moon just in time to remind me of a new month.

I retire into the warmth and comfort of our new camper van – HMExplorer 3 as I call it, christened after the two boats with same namesake in Myanmar and the Philippines. They all offer adequate comfort for the seasoned explorer in the field or at sea, providing a bit of decadence as I start reaching the end of my five decades of exploration.

At my age, I may not be as fit to pursue rivers to their various sources but being at a headstream and so close to yet another source is a good consolation prize.

Upper reaches of the Irtysh River / 額爾濟斯河上游

月適時提醒我，又是一個新的月份。

我返回我們舒服溫暖的新露營車——我稱它「HM 探險者 3 號」——緊接在緬甸與菲律賓的兩艘同名船之後。這些交通工具，無論在曠野或海上，總能為一群身經百戰的探險者提供絕佳的舒適空間，在我的探險生涯即將屆滿五十年之際，我稍稍縱容一下自己，難得躺平與頹廢。

到我這年紀，恐怕已無法再一一探索河川源頭，但能親臨一個巨河上游，而且離另一個源頭如此相近，那對我已是個很不錯的安慰獎了。

Felt rug artifacts / 毛氈地毯

阿爾泰山自然保護區的野生動物

# WILDLIFE OF THE ALTAY

Fuyun, Xinjiang – May 3, 2022

## WILLDLIFE OF THE ALTAY
### Snow Leopard, Ibex and rare Asiatic Beaver

*Chu Wen, at 27 years of age, is jumping with excitement as if she were between two and seven. "Come look, come look," she yells out at me, though I am barely a few steps away from her. She has just opened the front of a camera trap strapped to the top of a cement block pinnacle marking the end of an eighteen-kilometer dirt road.*

*"There are almost a thousand images recorded." The voice of excitement accelerated to an even higher pitch. "945 images to be exact. This trap was set up last October, before winter set in and the snow prevented anyone from coming in," she explained to me. As she was speaking, her finger was fast and busy on the rewind button to review the images taken. The entrance into this canyon is blocked by a metal gate, prohibiting entry in order to protect the drainage of the Irtysh River, which supplies water to Fuyun County. An exception has been made for us, due to the important wildlife work Chu Wen and her NGO are doing in the region.*

*The drive in, following the Irtysh, has been rough and bumpy, passing many areas with landslides and fallen rocks that barely allow for the width of our 4x4 to get through. There are four cars in our caravan, led by a Landcruiser fully converted for off-road use. Behind the wheels is Li Yunfei, a police officer who loves four-wheeling and knows this dirt road like no one else. Chu Wen has begged him to come along, promising me that Li's eyes are as sharp as nails, able to locate ibex mountain goat even high up on the crevices, as this river canyon is sandwiched between steep rugged hills. Indeed, he did not fail in this task.*

*But the camera trap would reveal what we humans cannot see so easily, or quite so closely. Among the first hundred or so images Chu Wen quickly scans through, there are plenty of pictures of the Asiatic Ibex, including some males with huge ridged horns. Those crescent-moon-like horns arch back into a sharp point, almost reaching the animal's mid body when the head is raised. I can just imagine that a large male would use it to scratch his itch as far as his back-end, besides using them to conquer another challenging male during rutting season.*

*But what draws Chu Wen's excitement is not the ibex. Those animals she has seen many times, and she has recorded their majestic looks in some of the finest ibex photographs I have ever seen. The ibex, regal as they may look, are only prey to another monarch of the high mountains. What draws the breath out of her mouth are the numerous images of Snow Leopard.*

*I can hear her "oohs and ahhs" as she reviews the photos recorded. The*

Chu Wen with camera trap /
初雯和自動監測相機

*frequency with which the Snow Leopard shows up is phenomenal; 57 photos; face shots, side views, back shots, etc., not only photos but occasional short flicks of video as well, 19 segments. Indeed, he, she, or it, was performing in front of the camera, posing here and there as if doing a fashion catwalk. A spotted cat pelt on a catwalk is no longer acceptable to a largely conservation-conscious fashion world. But to see it on a real cat doing the performance in nature is just wonderful. And that unmistakable long tail, bushy and spotted, swinging behind like a provocative and seductive boa, makes this cat a rightful claimant of flagship species status.*

*I have studied, photographed and written about many endangered species, prodding the public for their conservation. They included the Black-necked Crane, Tibetan Antelope, Wild Yak, Argali Sheep, Pied Snub-nosed Monkey, and more. But in almost five decades of exploration, this is the first time I have gotten so close to a Snow Leopard, standing on exactly the same spot where one has stood. And with the Asiatic Ibex, this is the first time I have seen them in the wild.*

*In just one afternoon through this little-known canyon, we have had five sightings of the ibex. The first three were viewed from far away, high up on the ridge where the cliff is, as the animal stood out as a tiny spot with two noticeable horns. They were somewhat small horns, thus it was likely a female on lookout, watching with curiosity our small caravan kicking up new dust. Each time, it was Li who spotted the animal and stopped the car to point out these little spots to me. Even so, my 300mm lens could barely make out the ibex among the hills.*

*At our fourth sighting, on our way driving back, I sent Zhou Laohu, our caver and cartographer, to* fly our drone up towards the ridge. It successfully came back with photos and video of a herd of the ibex, perhaps two dozen in number. In one instant, the drone caught a young ibex seated and relaxing. As the drone got closer, it rose in alarm and ran off into the distant hills.

Our last sighting was when we were only five kilometers from the entrance gate. By then, it was near eight in the evening. But with Xinjiang time some three hours behind Beijing, the sky was still fully lit. Li said that he expected the ibex would begin to come lower into the canyon, down to the riverbank to quench their thirst. Indeed, we ran right into a herd with even several baby goats heading down into the mid-hills. As we stopped, they began climbing higher again, but they allowed time for my camera to click and snap a few worthy shots. No longer just a silhouette, these few shots finally capture the ibex as they now have been imprinted into my mind as well.

Li told me that there are probably dozens of herds of ibex within this 18-kilometer canyon, probably one of the densest populations of this endangered animal anywhere to be seen, and within only 25 kilometers from the city of Fuyun. The largest herd he has ever come across was over 70 animals. I told Li and Chu Wen that I would

Snow Leopard facing camera / 雪豹正對相機　　Camera recorded ibex / 相機捕捉到北山羊　Snow Leopard with bushy tail / 雪豹毛茸茸的尾巴

A female ibex / 母北山羊
Two female ibex / 兩隻母北山羊

certainly return, perhaps quite soon during another season, when the canyon would not only be filled with these rare and photogenic wildlife, but also with the full colors of the autumn foliage.

For a moment, my thoughts fell into an abyss of another world. If there was an imaginary global map of the natural and animal world, this eighteen-kilometer gorge might become a tiny country called Ibexastan. Perhaps nearby just within another hundred kilometers might be another country stretched along one singular river and called Beaverstan. That may be too farfetched; maybe just a Disneyland-like town called Beaverstown. Suddenly, I feel I am not 72, but 27, or two to seven, like Chu Wen.

Unlike the ibex, which I am seeing for the first time, the Asiatic Beaver is another Class One protected animal of China that I got a chance to meet almost twenty years ago. In fact, this wonderful aquatic mammal has become quite intimate with CERS, as we even made a short film about them. The story however, traces back to Chu Wen's father, Chu Hongjun.

It was 2001 when I was in northern Xinjiang and first heard about the Asiatic Beaver. They live along just one river, the Ulungur, which flows down from the Mongolian People's Republic into China. Trying to enter the nature reserve, newly established to protect the beaver, I was turned away. In keeping with my past practice, I quickly devised a plan to help support research and conservation of the animal by providing some seed money. That is how I met Chu Hongjun, then a biologist studying both the Argali Sheep and the beaver. That led to my return in 2003 with Chu guiding me to observe both the Argali and beaver.

Now twenty years later, Hongjun's daughter Chu Wen has grown from a little girl to be a wildlife biologist and conservationist in her own right, founding her own NGO focused on study and protection of the Asiatic Beaver, as well as operating a successful wildlife rescue center.

While the Beaver Reserve is funded and operated by government, Chu Wen took on protecting the larger population of the beaver, outside the reserve but inhabiting the same Ulungur river system. The reserve has recorded a population of 38 beaver families, usually with an average of four members to each "nest-hold", whereas Chu Wen's group now has tallied 159 beaver families, about four folds in total, outside of the reserve that need as much, if not more, protection.

Organizing support from local Kazak communities, her programs have now received nation-wide support. With her new nickname "Beaver Princess," given by her fans and followers on the internet, her work has garnered so much attention among China's younger generation that she has been given many accolades. The pinnacle of her achievements so far is representing China's youth in delivering a keynote speech at last year's UN COP15

Beaver photos taken by Chu Wen / 初雯拍攝的河狸

「中國探險學會」與初紅軍的連結，搭起了一座橋，帶領我們走進河狸世界，也與初雯建立起相知相惜的關係。初雯堅持要向我學習，因她從小便以我送她給父親的著作當教材，當她啟發的導師。但我不斷提醒她，發自內心的熱情，屬於右腦的功能；而知識與技能則是外來的刺激，那是左腦的運作。我鼓勵她要持續發揮左腦潛力來支持她的右腦，讓她心中熾烈的熱情，像光與熱，成為照耀與感染他人的驅動力；至於聰明才智，要把它當掌舵的副手，用來排除阻撓前進的障礙。

我也和初雯分享我這三十多年來投身非政府組織的經驗，和觀察他人所累積的反思。我們談論募款方案與財務要如何謹慎管理。一般來說，小規模的非政府組織個人化色彩較濃厚，可以保有更純粹的理想，主體性格鮮明；而大規模的組織則偏向企業管理經營化，通常更像品牌創造，必須在數字上下功夫，我們稱之為典型的「影響力」。小組織著重的是個人故事與敘述，大組織關注的是格式與圖表，以及更多數字化的資料。兩者都各有其不可取代的優勢，要如何在大小組織之間做選擇，或在兩者之間找出最適合她、兩者兼具的混合型組織，考驗她的智慧。我提醒她，有些非政府組織如「庫斯托協會」(Cousteau Society)、「李基基金會」(Leakey Foundation) 與「珍古德基金會」(Goodall Foundation)，雖然都是個人色彩濃厚的非政府組織，但經營得有聲有色，對世界的影響力不容小覷。

某日午後，初雯帶我重訪河狸。我們屏氣凝神地靜坐於烏倫古河畔的巢穴旁，巢穴有個長長的出入口通道，宛如蓋在水中的河狸水壩。初紅軍也帶著兩個研究生遠道而來陪伴我們。

夕陽西下，久別重逢的老友相談甚歡。聊著聊著，紅軍忽然招手叫我到他的隱秘的位置。我朝他手指方向望去，一隻成年雄河狸從水裡冒出頭來，河面上泛起小小漣漪，隨即見牠悠然游向對岸。彷彿才一眨眼功夫，河狸已經爬上岸，看來是飢腸轆轆了，只見牠迫不及待啃咬一根新鮮樹枝，把樹枝帶到水岸邊，準備大快朵頤，享受晚餐。說不定那是牠的「早餐」呢，畢竟牠很可能才剛從漫長的冬眠中醒來，一睜開眼，便是天色漸晚的春日黃昏。

我轉身一看，初雯正拿著相機與長鏡頭，不停地連番按下快門。那台相機恰似撮合戀情的媒人，「河狸公主」忙著和她心愛的「河狸王子」共譜浪漫約會。也或許她是個偷拍的狗仔隊，跟著她的導師，有樣學樣了。

Ibex herd / 北山羊群

情牽哈薩克四十年

# AN UPDATE ON FORTY YEARS OF KAZAK ENCOUNTERS

Fuyun, Xinjiang - May 3, 2022

## AN UPDATE ON FORTY YEARS OF KAZAK ENCOUNTERS
### *Version 1.0 to 5.0 plus some provocative ranting*

*Today is the first day marking the end of Ramadan, a very important date for Muslims worldwide. Fasting has ended, feasting has just begun. For me it is just as important, as I celebrate my career-long involvement with the Muslim world that began forty years ago; involvement to such an extent that I have written a book on Islam in China, and produced an expanded updated version, published in the UK in 1990 and 2011 respectively. That perhaps allows me to claim myself an old-hand on the topic.*

*My first encounter with Kazaks, one of ten Muslim nationalities of China, was in 1982 when I led an expedition to study the minority groups of China for the National Geographic. Subsequently, pictures of a Kazak wedding and a Kazak nomadic family moving camp were published in my article in the magazine. Even before that, as a young journalist, I had already first visited China's Muslim region of Xinjiang as early as 1979.*

*Unlike others who have taken a sudden and peripheral interest in Chinese Muslims and China's western region, my involvement and observations on this topic and geographic area span several decades. Perhaps I am justified to speak on the subject.*

Kazak moving camp in 1982 / 哈薩克族遷徙 1982 年

*To mark the end of Ramadan, a local horse-racing event is held at Fuyun, the heart of the Kazak community in northern Xinjiang. Fuyun County within Altay Prefecture has about 70,000 Kazak among its 100,000 population. There are close to 1.8 million Kazaks in China, of which around 350,000 reside in Altay Prefecture. Events and festivities like horse-racing have been suspended for two years due to the pandemic and this one has been reinstated only this year as Covid is largely under control here.*

*We arrived at 10am, long before the event which was to start around noon. The "modern" racecourse comes with grandstand and spectator areas, and a circular dirt track of 1600 meters. After we occupied the best seats at the top of the grandstand, I went off to the open ground where the horses and their riders were preparing for the showdown. Pick-up trucks continuously drove in with horses standing gracefully on the flatbed, most with colorful overcoats over their bodies. We picked out a couple of the young riders (they were all young riders, in their early teens) to talk to.*

families were exiled to faraway Turkey, we obtained multiple copies of the book *Kazak Exodus* for our library in Hong Kong.

*Xinjiang is among China's 23 provinces and 5 autonomous regions in a diverse multi-ethnic country. China has 56 nationalities, a few more than a deck of cards. Today both these regions and ethnicities have become a set of cards with which to trump China. We have seen the Tibet and Tibetan cards played for decades, and now the Xinjiang and Uighur cards. If there are Guangdong and Sichuan cards, Mongolian and Manchu cards, they will certainly be used, in the future.*

*In today's world of big data, people are used to dealing with big numbers, like recently the number "one million" Uighur being thrown around arbitrarily. I trust my small number of two families of Kazak are more reliable. Ironically, some twenty years ago, CERS organized students from the Hong Kong International School and counterparts in Xinjiang to produce two decks of cards, one featuring Tibet's endangered animals and the other Xinjiang's. I believe such projects, small as they are, are more productive and positive.*

*Maybe to some people in the West, my personal observations are somewhat counter-productive and inconvenient. But one of the cases we interviewed*

Kazak festival at Yili 2001 / 哈薩克節慶在伊犁於 2001 年

*in the geological park of Koktokay perhaps speak much about current government policy as opposed to birth-control policy of the past. Ku'er Man is 29 years of age. She married her husband in 2016 and her son, now five years old, was born a year later in 2017. In answer to call by government to have more children, she is now pregnant with a second child, expecting in June this year. In fact, she stated that the government encourages minority nationalities to have even more than two children.*

*During the Cultural Revolution, which I had the opportunity to observe during my early years in China, this huge country of over 1 billion was largely irrelevant to the US and the rest of the world. Cuba, while a small country, was closer and more relevant to the US then. But China's rise in the 21st Century turned the world around.*

*At first the West was so focused on using China's cheap labor to advance their primary economic interests that China's rise was accepted. Now, it is seen as a cause for alarm, and the most urgent matter is to stop its rise; peaceful rise or not is irrelevant. To smear China as expansionist and with a hegemonic agenda is the best way to create a "united front" against its rise.*

*Thus, many reporters in the West are now all too eager to discover singular stories to portray a grim and pessimistic picture of China. I prefer to sit at a streetside café and restaurant to observe quietly, especially the faces of older folks and children, whose eyes and smiles are more telling than so-called "personal" stories.*

*I do not have a foreign name attached to a branded media conglomerate to provide "cover" as a neutral and authentic voice. But speaking of cards, my calling card is having done a stint as frontline journalist for the National Geographic in the 1980s, honored by Time Magazine as one of their 25 Asian Heroes in 2002, as a front-page story in the Wall Street Journal, and over the years being featured on CNN over a dozen times, besides Discovery and Aljazeera Channels. Some may say those are in the past and has passed its expiration date. But, my stories are based on first-hand observations, from over four decades of travel as well as my most current experience.*

*So here I share my experience and my opinion, a Xinjiang version 5.0, as compared to those version 1.0 popular among the West today. My consolation is that my long-time select friends in the West trust my observations and encourage me to continue producing our exploration reports, whether they coincide with mainstream speculations and beliefs or not.*

Kazak, HM & guests 1997 / 哈薩克族，HM 和客人於 1997 年

# 情牽哈薩克四十年

## 從 1.0 至 5.0 的版本更新——外加一份豪言壯語

今天是結束齋戒月的第一天，也是全球穆斯林最重要的節日。忍飢受餓的齋戒結束，盛宴即將登場。對我來說，這一天也同樣重要，因為我也要為自己四十年前深入穆斯林世界，與他們建立夥伴關係而歡喜慶祝——我全心參與，最終還撰寫了一本關於中國伊斯蘭教的書、且更新再版，於一九九〇與二〇一一年兩度在英國出版——由此可見我投入穆斯林世界之深。如果說，我對這議題較一些專家多所認識，應該也不為過。

一九八二年，我帶領《國家地理雜誌》考察隊展開中國少數民族的研究，由此而第一次接觸哈薩克族人——中國的十大穆斯林族群之一。之後，一場哈薩克的婚禮與哈薩克牧民遷移帳篷的照片，隨著我的報導刊載於雜誌上。其實在這之前，雖然只是初出茅廬的年輕記者，我早在一九七九年便已首次進入中國的新疆穆斯林區域採訪。

有些人或許一時興起，帶有目的性而突然對中國的穆斯林和中國西部地區關心起來，但我的狀況比較不同，我對這些議題的熱衷與觀察，包括對這地域的鑽研，已持續了數十年；或許這些累積的經驗讓我能針對這議題，合情合理地表達我的觀感。

為了紀念齋戒月的結束，位於新疆北部哈薩克社區中心的富蘊縣，一場賽馬活動正式揭幕。阿爾泰地區內的富蘊縣，十萬人口中，哈薩克人占了七萬。中國境內將近一百八十萬哈薩克人，其中定居於阿爾泰地區的哈薩克人有三十萬人之多。哈薩克的當地節慶與類似賽馬等傳統賽事，已因新冠疫情而停辦兩年，還好今年的疫情控制得宜，期盼已久的活動才得以重新開放與舉辦。

我們早上十點抵達當地，距離中午才開始的活動還有一段時間。這個「現代化」的賽馬場不僅有看台區與觀眾席，還有一條一千六百公尺的環狀土路作跑道。先找到看台區，佔好最上層的絕佳好位，然後，我才安心走到開放區；那裡是專為騎士與他們的馬打造的備戰區。一台台敞篷皮卡陸續開進來，車後載著駿馬良駒，披著五顏六色的外衣，英姿煥發而優雅。我們認識了幾位看來只有十幾歲的少年騎士。

巴赫加納提 (Bahejia Nati)，綽號「小巴」的騎士，今年只有十二歲，在離富蘊縣三十公里左右的哈拉通科 (Hala Tongke) 村一間小學就讀六年級。小巴四歲時，由於幼兒園和小學之間相距五公里，他和大四歲的哥哥學會騎馬，即使嚴寒冬日，也鞍馬勞頓去上學。小小年紀便過起了策馬奔騰的日子，哥哥烏拉哈迪 (Wula Hati) 因而練就一身好功夫，成了過去幾年賽馬活動的冠軍高手。今天，這位常勝軍的村里生活，已經大為改善，「騎馬上學」不復存在，取而代之的，是四輪的校車準時來接送孩子到學校。小巴十九歲的姊姊娜孜依納 (Nazi Yi'na)，今年已開始就讀阿克蘇大學一年級。

Kazak family today / 今日的哈薩克家族

Racing to finish / 奔向終點
Horses rounding corner / 賽馬於彎道上

Kazak girl and yurt in 1982 / 哈薩克小女孩和哈薩克包於 1982 年

Exercise machine / 訓練機器

二〇一九年，當小巴九歲時，他開始參加賽馬，而且屢創佳績，總是名列前茅。今天的比賽，小巴一如以往，不負家人的高度期待，在三十名參賽騎手中脫穎而出，在三千公尺的比賽項目中排名第三。小巴帶回家的不只是榮譽，還有獎金三千人民幣。總計九場的賽馬活動，吸引超過四十位年齡介於十一至十七歲的年輕騎士參加，參賽選手都打著赤膊，沒有戴上馬鞍，以最質樸無華的方式，快馬騎乘，叱吒衝刺。算起來，參與各種競賽的駿馬，至少超過一百五十匹。

以小巴的家庭來說，他們家有三十頭牛、六十隻羊與令人耳目一新的三十匹好馬；除了牲畜以外，還有三台機車、一部電動單車與汽車。每一年，至少有八至十五匹小馬出生，家人通常會把兩三隻有潛力成為良駒的小馬保留起來，其餘的則以四至五千人民幣賣出。一般來說，狀況最好的一歲馬，可以賣到一萬人民幣，而兼具各方優勢的成年馬——介於七至八歲不等——身價甚至高達五至七萬人民幣。小巴個人擁有四批小馬，他經常在假期時到他們的夏季牧場騎馬，駕馭自如的馬術和人馬之間的默契，隨著他的成長而不斷精進；今天這隻為他贏得賽事的好馬是「昭覺惹克」，哈薩克文原意是「無畏」。

除了獎金，小巴的父親也因兒子的不凡成就而自掏腰包加碼三百元獎勵兒子。小巴要用這筆錢買幾件衣服、書籍與文具。他難掩自豪地說，他的儲蓄筒已經存了兩千五百多元，這筆數字對一個小男孩來說，相當可觀。不過，他並不滿足於此，一心期待有朝一日贏得一台皮卡車或拖拉機的頭等大獎。

我們在新疆北部逗留一週，這段時間總共在不同地方採訪與探視了九個哈薩克家庭。這些訪談都是臨時起意的行動，視當時的狀況，保持彈性的選擇與決定。我在此特別提及兩則訪談紀錄，以此為例，說明北新疆哈薩克的現狀。其餘更詳盡的研究與介紹，則是為了「中國探險學會」而做，也都紀錄在案。

Neighbor's grandson / 鄰居的孫子

我們訪視的第一個哈薩克家庭，是哈維古莉 (Hayi Na'er Guli)，她家就在我們觀察亞洲河狸不遠處的地方。四十三歲的古莉，二十三年前和丈夫結婚後，育有一子——今年二十歲的拉錫別克 (Lazi Bieke)。拉錫別克不久前從職訓學校回歸故里，協助放牧的家族工作。古莉還有一名十二歲的女兒吳樂江 (Wule Jiang)，特別活潑外向、快言快語，不斷自願想當我們的翻譯。這個家庭養了二十頭牛，十五隻羊和三十「峰」駱駝。聽聞他們以「峰」當駱駝量詞，令我倍感好奇，這麼說來，背上隆起兩個駝峰的亞洲駱駝，理當以雙倍加乘來計算。

每年五月至九月，一家人便拔營往高處遷居，搬往一百五十公里以外的夏天牧場。過去，他們需要耗費一週時間才能把所有牲畜帶到牧場，但今時不同往日，他們可以租台卡車，只要舟車勞頓一日，人畜都能就定位，好好安頓。

古莉家的年收入介於六萬至七萬人民幣之間。這筆收入源自乳牛的出售，每年估計可賣五、六頭牛。一般來說，每一頭小牛犢能賣到六千元，而成年牛則能賣到一萬元左右。至於駱駝，大小售價差別不大，每一頭成年駱駝大約是兩萬人民幣。古莉家養了十二頭成年母駱駝，五歲時便已發育完成並能產奶，每頭駱駝一天產奶量是二至五公斤，每公斤售價約三十元。這季節適逢產奶高峰期，古莉一週內便可累積多達五十公斤的駱駝奶。駱駝一身是寶，駝毛的價值每公斤四十人民幣。過去數年來，由於政府實施「退牧還草」的政策，為了彌補牧民，每個牧民家庭一年可獲兩萬人民幣的津貼補助。

哈薩克婦女天生一雙巧手，尤其手作的羊毛毯，技藝高明；那些精緻繁複的設計與圖案，標識她們各不相同的身分。一般來說，一百隻羊的羊毛原料才足夠編織一張全尺寸的地毯。這些地毯款式與設計別出心裁，無論鋪在地上或高掛牆上，或覆蓋在高腳床鋪上，怎麼看都是一件華冠麗服。哈薩克家庭也會另外為未出嫁的女兒精心製作毛毯，有朝一日當女兒結婚時的嫁妝。其他譬如一些特殊場合，哈薩克家庭也會把獨一無二的地毯當禮物，送給特殊關係的親戚或友人。

我開口詢問古莉，可否為我們新設的新疆館蒐集一些哈薩克獨有的毛毯當展示品。古莉二話不說，隨即挑選兩張較舊的小毛毯送給我們。我又驚又喜，心想自己不過是個恰巧路過的陌生人，卻讓主人以厚禮相待，這已足以說明哈薩克人對其他族群慷慨大方的民族性。受寵若驚的我們，頓覺不好意思，於是決定向她買兩張大一點的毛毯，而且一改過去買前殺價的習慣，以表謝意。

自一九八二年以來，為了拍攝與採訪需求，我經常到類似蒙古包的哈薩克氈房裡住宿。在那些年間接觸過的受訪對象，包括青海的格爾木、新疆的巴里坤，以及二〇〇一至二〇〇三年在新疆北部的大片區域，一直延伸到俄羅斯與哈薩克邊境的伊犁與喀納斯湖。此次遠行至北新疆，也是一趟更新過去遊歷的經驗。

回想一九九四至二〇〇五的十年間，「中國探險學會」在敦煌附近成立據點，就在距離甘肅省西北部的阿克塞縣不遠，方便我們探索這個以哈薩克族為主體的少數民族自治縣，進行許多研究工作。我們甚至曾邀請兩位哈薩克族朋友到香港訪問。為了深入研究一九三〇年代、那段發生於哈薩克族人被流放至遙遠土耳其的悲慘歷史，我們還特別為香港的圖書館收集了不同版本的書籍《哈薩克出走》(Kazak Exodus)，留下相關的歷史紀錄與文獻。

新疆是中國二十三個省與五個自治區之一；身為多元民族的大國，其中五十六個民族已比一副撲克牌還多。今天，這些區域與民族也已成為一套國外用以打擊中國的王牌。我們見證了西藏與藏族這張打了十幾年的牌，輪番上陣的還有新疆和維吾爾族這張牌。如果未來，廣東與四川、蒙古與滿族也各手握一副牌，他們肯定也會被慫恿出牌。

生活在今天的大數據世界，人人已習於和大數據打交道，譬如近期與維吾爾族相關的「一百萬」議題，便是個有意無意被一再提起的數據。但我相信我親身相處的「兩個」哈薩克家庭的小數據，更可靠實在。我還記得大約二十年前，「中國探險學會」曾號召「香港國際學校」的一些學生，和新

With Kazak of Barkol Xinjiang 1996 / 新疆巴里坤的哈薩克族於 1996 年

Kazak of Lake Kanas 2001 / 哈薩克族於喀納斯湖於 2001 年

疆的夥伴共同合作，製作了兩幅牌卡，分別是西藏與新疆的瀕危物種。我深信，如此群策群力的合作動物保育計畫，雖然規模小，但更具成效與正面意義。

或許對一些西方世界的人來說，我的個人觀感可能顯得適得其反與不合時宜。然而，也許我們在北疆的可可托海 (Koktokay) 地質公園的一個採訪案例，可以說明目前的政府宣導與過去的節育政策之間，如何迥然有別。二十九歲的庫爾嫚，二〇一六年結婚，婚後隔年年底生下兒子，今年五歲。為了響應鼓勵生育的政策，她現在已順利懷上第二個孩子，預產期是今年六月。她坦然直言，政府其實很鼓勵少數民族多生育，若能超過兩胎會更好。

文化大革命期間，我曾有機會近距離觀察早期的中國，這個擁有十多億人口的大國幾乎自絕於美國和世界其他國家，兩不相干；以當時的國際情勢來看，就連小國如古巴，也能對美國更重要及令他關心，而當時的中國，根本望塵莫及。然而，二十一世紀的中國崛起後，已徹底扭轉世界局勢。

一開始，西方國家專心利用中國的廉價勞動力，以提升自身的主要經濟利益；中國崛起，初步已獲各方接受，但曾幾何時，這現狀卻被視為警示之源，大家的當務之急竟是想辦法阻撓它的崛起；至於是否和平崛起，已不重要。誣衊中國以霸權手段行使擴張主義，已成為各方壓制中國崛起最有力的「統一戰線」。

於是，許多西方世界的記者，也一窩蜂熱衷於挖掘各種奇聞軼事，對中國極盡污名之能事，把它描繪成可驚可怖的殘酷大國。至於我，我比較喜歡獨坐街邊的咖啡館與餐廳裡，靜看所有人事物，我尤其喜歡觀察那些老人與孩子的面容，簡直令我著迷，他們的眼神與笑顏所傳達的故事，遠比所謂誇誇其詞的「個人」抹黑敘事，更有說服力。

我沒有一個掛在著名媒體的外國姓名，沒有外國記者能以主流集團來「掩護」所謂中立與真實可靠的報導。不過，如果說起名片，那或許最能代表我的標誌是一九八〇年代擔任過《國家地理雜誌》的前線記者、二〇〇二年獲選為《時代週刊》的二十五位「亞洲英雄」之一，也曾被《華爾街日報》當封面故事報導，多年來也在有線電視 CNN、《探索頻道》與「半島電視」報導了無數次。也許有人會說，那些都是塵封已久的往事，早已過了有效期。但我的文字與故事都源自第一手的觀察，歷經四十年深入現場的採訪，與最近期的當前體驗。

因此，我特別在這裡分享我《新疆 5.0 版本更新》的經歷與觀點，以抗衡當今流行於西方世界的 1.0 版本。這過程中最令我欣慰的，是我在西方國家裡的老朋友對我的信任，他們選擇相信我的觀察，無論這些內容是否符合主流的推測與信念，他們仍鼓勵我繼續把探索的報告與紀錄，公諸於世。

芝
麻
開
門

# OPEN SESAME

Bulunkou, Xinjiang – May 20, 2022

HM expedition 1984 / HM1984 年的探險

7649-meter Kongur Tagh / 7649 公尺高的公格爾峰

中國帕米爾高原上的塔吉克人

# A TAJIK ON THE CHINESE PAMIRS

Pamirs, Xinjiang – May 18, 2022

## *A TAJIK ON THE CHINESE PAMIRS*

*In Tibet, I would call it karma.  But here in the high Pamirs, it must be the will of Allah that we met with Bijiang Bige Wazi, totally by chance.  His humble demeanor and mild smile can be deceiving, as he is recognized as a non-material cultural heritage holder among the Tajik, a nationality of China speaking a language in the Persian family.*

*Our team of eight is cruising on the road in a caravan of three cars, heading toward the Pakistan/ Afghan border with China.  It has been a most beautiful drive with snow-capped mountains marching along with us as escorts on both sides.  I called out on our radio for the lead car to pull to the side where there seems to be a rest area.*

*We pulled to a stop, but the toilet was locked.  Understandable, since so few people pass this way, especially since all cross-border traffic came to a halt when the pandemic started.  Below the road was a fenced area with a pre-fab house and a pre-fab yurt, no longer made of felt but of canvas.  A small car was parked outside and the chimney was fuming smoke.  Momentarily, a man with army camouflaged hat and jacket came out to check on the noise we had created.*

*Bijiang, 42 years of age, is no ordinary man on the Pamirs, the word meaning "Roof of the World."*

Pre-fab yurt / 組合式蒙古包

With deep eye-sockets and a long hooked nose like an eagle's beak, he is a special member of the 50,000 Tajik of China, who live mainly near the Pakistan/Afghan border. They are the only Shiite Muslims in China. The rest of the nine groups of Chinese Muslims are all Suni's.

Bijiang is not only modest, he is on the margin of being shy. It took some prompting as we questioned him about some action photos on the wall of his yurt to realize that he is the main organizer of a very special traditional sport on this high plateau. Buz kashi, called "Duo Yang" in Chinese, is the favorite sport among Kazaks and Kirgiz of Central Asia. Two teams would race on horseback tugging violently on a sheep or goat pelt and the successful contestant would deposit the trophy on a designated spot. Bijiang, however, is now the inheritor and organizer of a similar sport, using yaks rather than on horses.

I can finally see the pride in Bijiang's eyes as he tells us that the sport's history at Tuxkorgan can be traced back to

Proud with his awards / 自豪得到許多獎項
With his hand drum / 他的手鼓

the second century BC. Yaks are used not only as livestock, but as beasts of burden here on the Pamirs. Each year between the months of June and September when herders converge at their summer pasture, the "Duo Yang" pass-time gradually became a popular sports event. In time, it became an event performed during festivities and even during wedding celebrations.

Bijiang began learning Buz kashi on yak from his father at the age of 14 as the third generation of organizers since his grandfather's days. Recently, his ten-years-old son Yibimen Bijiang also started participating in his first such event. This has served as the young boy's symbol of reaching adulthood; his coming of age.

Within the county of Tuxkorgan, Bijiang now has 40 Tajik students learning from him the skills and regulations of this sport. Each year in June, he would gather them at the summer pasture and train them to compete. He has set up two yurts at the site so as to also entertain visitors and tourists. Since 2019, he has organized over 20 competitions each summer, and performed for close to a thousand spectators in one year. This year however, due to the pandemic, he has managed to organize such events only twice, and only during their own Tajik festivities.

Bijiang is also a member of the civilian border patrol, guarding the high border of Khunjrap with Pakistan. He began this dual-career in 2000 and has spent a good part of 22 years posting at various stations along the border. Each month, he and 15 to 20 of his team spend 15 days on rotational guard duties. It comes with a stipend, and room and board are provided. Since his grandfather's time, his family has been members of the border patrol team. Back then, his grandfather did it to play his patriotic role with no stipend at all. Today, with his livestock sales, his yak event, and border patrol role, altogether Bijiang can derive an income of close to one million RMB annually, not a small sum for someone living in the farthest inland corner of China.

As the main person still active in this rare sport, Bijiang has been recognized among the Tajik in 2014 as "holder of

Buz kashi game on yak / 犛牛上的叼牛比賽

Bijiang & wife with HM / 畢江夫妻和 HM

畢江侃侃談起塔什庫爾干 (Tuxkorgan) 這項年代久遠的傳統運動，當他把時間軸往後追溯到公元前二世紀時，我瞥見他發亮的眼神中，難掩自豪。在帕米爾高原上，犛牛不只是家畜，也要背負重物。每年六月至九月，當牧民拔營遷徙至夏季牧場時，為了打發漫漫夏日，「叼羊」逐漸成了最受歡迎的全民運動；久而久之，運動成了特殊節慶的活動，甚至出現於婚禮客串上。

畢江十四歲時，開始跟著父親坐在犛牛背上學「叼羊」，一躍而成為祖父時代以來的第三代活動策劃者。最近，畢江自己的十歲小兒依比門‧畢江，也躍躍欲試，摩拳擦掌，準備參加他生涯首次「叼羊」活動。事實上，這項活動已成為當地男孩「轉大人」的符號；一個象徵成年禮的標誌。

在塔什庫爾干縣，畢江身邊至少跟了四十名塔吉克徒弟，他們向師傅學習「犛牛背上叼羊」的運動技能與競賽規則。每年六月，他召聚所有徒弟，以比賽為目標，在夏季牧場訓練他們。他在現場搭建兩個蒙古包，訓練同時，不忘隨時接待訪客與旅人。自二〇一九年起，畢江每年夏天都如期舉辦「犛牛上的叼羊賽」，至今已辦了超過二十場，每年吸引近千名絡繹不絕的觀眾。今年例外，雖然疫情肆虐，他還是想方設法辦了兩場，但只能在塔吉克的節慶期

Buz Kazi competition on yaks / 犛牛上進行叼羊比賽

間舉辦。

畢江同時也是民間邊境巡邏隊一員，守護紅其拉甫山口 (Khunjrap) 與巴基斯坦之間的國界。畢江從二〇〇〇年身兼雙職至今，他在這段長達二十二年的時間裡，曾被派往邊界上的各個駐點。畢江和團隊裡的十五至二十名同僚每個月花十五天時間輪流執行巡防任務。這是有額外津貼的服務，而且還提供食宿福利。從祖父母的那一代開始，畢江的家人就一直從事邊境巡邏的工作；差別在於，老人家是出於愛國情懷，即時沒有津貼也盡忠職守。今天，靠著出售牲畜、舉辦犛牛活動與邊境巡邏等收入，畢江的年收入可達一百萬人民幣左右，這樣的金額對一個中國最偏遠內陸山區的居民來說，已算不少。

畢江因為持續堅持舉辦這項獨特少見的傳統運動，而在二〇一四年被塔吉克族推舉為「非物質文化遺產持有人」。二〇一九年，這份榮譽再受喀什區的縣級單位認可，捷報頻傳。不僅眾望所歸，畢江也因此而獲得每年四千八百元的特別獎勵金。在現場的我，也分享了畢江的成就，以他為榮。我們往來幾回「拉鋸」後，當然，不是為羊皮囊，而是幾番交涉協商，我終於成功說服畢江把比賽用的犛牛鞍氈賣給我，讓我可以把無比珍貴的塔吉克文物收藏品帶回家。

從一九八四及一九九三年兩次探索中國帕米爾高原至今，歲月如流，一轉眼已過三、四十年。如今舊地重訪，心頭湧上許多美好的記憶。當年那個世代，要到如此偏遠的邊境不只考驗遠途千里的勞累，還要面對翻山渡水的顛簸路況。我記得過程中何止動用四輪驅動的車子，還騎過馬，甚至背負一身沈重的探險裝備騎著駱駝慢行一段長路。

今天，能在此與畢江偶遇，我覺得特別欣慰。一如我經常對身邊年輕人所說的，能有這些機會遊歷世界、探索各地，是多麼難能可貴的經驗；「你既已看過這些地方，這些地方是否也看見你了？」這趟旅途，我滿載而歸；不只帶走畢江收藏的照片與犛牛鞍氈，也結識了一位特別的塔吉克朋友，他是一位「把舊時代延伸到今天，讓古老傳統重現當下並帶到未來」的人——有幸認識畢江，令我欣喜不已。

Tajik wedding 1984 / 塔吉克族婚禮於 1984 年

A Tajik yurt 1993 / 塔吉克族的蒙古包於 1993 年

飛天魔毯，帶我重返往日時光

# BACK IN TIME WITH A FLYING CARPET

Kashi/Kashgar, Xinjiang – May 23, 2022

## BACK IN TIME WITH A FLYING CARPET

*I found a flying carpet that takes me back through time, to twenty years ago when we turned a new millennium, then back to the 1990s, then 1980s, and even as far back as the late 1970s when I first visited Xinjiang.*

*Abdul Wahab was not even born then. He is 36 years of age now. His shiny bald head and partially shaved chin make him seem much older. Thin and tall, his Uighur/Turkic look and frequent uttering of a few English words could easily disguise him as a foreigner. But Abdul is owner of one of the finest and best-known carpet shops in Old Town Kashgar. Today better known as Kashi, it was historically known as the crossroad of Central Asia on the Silk Road.*

*Since childhood, Abdul was groomed to love carpets. His father started the business some forty years ago by going to the countryside and purchasing select old carpets, cleaning them, then selling to foreign tourists. In those days, tourists arrived in droves as China opened up to the West. Around the year 2000, his father moved the carpet shop into Old Town Kashgar. As a teenager, Abdul started helping his father in the shop.*

*Gradually their carpets became better known and, through others' introductions, business*

Old Town Abdul's carpet shop / 老城區阿杜的地毯店          Abdul in shop / 在店裡的阿杜

prospered.  Many carpets were sold overseas to Europe and America.  Later, his father got to know a Pakistani merchant and began importing carpets from Pakistan and Afghanistan.  These were all 100% sheep wool or camel hair, more colorful, woven better than local carpets with ornamental motifs, and all crafted by hand.

By 2006, Abdul has full of confidence and opened his own carpet shop in Sanlitun, the hot bar district of Beijing.  He closed that profitable shop in 2016 after marrying his wife from Guilin and returned to Kashgar to rejoin his father's business.  In 2021, his father passed away due to a heart problem, and his wife went her separate way.

Today, Abdul's carpets are sourced from Afghanistan, Uzbekistan (mainly embroidered), Turkmenistan, Indian Kashmir, Iran, Pakistan, and even Egypt.  There are also some rare ones from Hotan of Xinjiang.  Those from foreign countries are usually shipped first to Pakistan, then through logistics companies, arrive in Taxkorgan in the Pamirs and finally to Kashgar.  But since 2020, due to the pandemic and the closing of all border entry points, no

Old Town noodles maker / 老城區的製麵者

new stock can arrive.

In the beginning, from 2001 to 2005, his father would go to Pakistan to check on his merchandise, take delivery and order future lots. As trust was built, the carpet merchants would instead come to Kashgar yearly between the months of May and October. They would take the order and have them produced mostly in Afghanistan where labor cost was much lower, supply of raw material more abundant, and quality higher. By April or May of the following year, the orders would be filled and ready to deliver to Kashi and onward to customers in China or overseas.

During a good year, their one shop can buy from 400,000 to half a million RMB worth of carpets and net a healthy profit. Today, even though the market has cooled a lot, his usual return is still around one million or more. Many of his customers know a lot about carpets and are very picky. More recently, due to both pandemic and travel restrictions, most of his customers are now from within China. When tour groups arrive, Abdul gives a commission to the tour guide, thus high-end tours often end at his door.

Old Town shops / 老城區的店舖

At the moment, his highest priced carpet in this two-storied shop is a locally woven carpet from Hotan with weave of between 500-600 dao per square meter. It is for sale at 250,000 RMB. A smaller one from Hotan, woven from mulberry silk, and another seventy-year-old carpet from Turkmenistan are both marked at over 100,000 RMB. The mulberry silk raw material is getting difficult to come by and each square meter is woven with 1200 dao, equivalent to needle point, for which labor is intensive, and hence price expensive.

When asked what he would pick as a gift for his best friend, Abdul answered without a thought; "Definitely a Xinjiang one, as I am from Xinjiang." We ended up purchasing a few carpets and rugs, including some I intend to give to friends who have helped us over the years.

As I rose to leave, I asked Abdul about my favorite place in Kashgar - Gaotai, a community on risen ground some twenty minutes' walk from Old Town. While Old Town is globally famous, few know of Gaotai, this ancient enclave where locals have lived for centuries. "I used to go there a lot as a kid and hang out with my friends, but no more," said Abdul. "The government has moved everyone out of the area and intends on making that place into yet another tourist site," he added.

It brought back a lot of old memories and images of when I spent time photographing this very unique place many years ago. It is hugely unfortunate, but such old adobe and wooden houses, without running water, toilets and proper plumbing, are considered unfit for families of our modern day. Indeed, it may feel quaint to those of us from elsewhere, but local young people are eager to embrace a more modern lifestyle.

*I can only reminisce about the past, as if flying my magic carpet. Or I can fast-rewind to revisit many of the images that are both imprinted in my mind and stored in my computer. It again makes me realize how important our documentation work is, recording much that is being eclipsed or is already lost. Hopefully, our archive and exhibits will help reveal past history and glory.*

*Next door to Abdul's carpet shop is a music store, selling a large selection of kumuzi, a guitar like instrument with a long thin neck and a small resonance box. There is also a huge collection of hand drums, large and small, with many having python-skin drumheads, said to produce the best quality sound.*

*Next is the corner of the square where many shops, snack food joints and antique venders converge. Two stairs on each side lead up to a balcony platform like a small theater with a restaurant behind. On the platform are two small tables for guests to sit and look out into the square or listen to a music performance by two or three local musicians. This has become my favorite spot to have a beer and listen to the drum and kumuzi. As is true anywhere in Xinjiang where the Uighur live, once the sound of the drum is heard, a dance may follow. So, it is here*

Images of Gaotai in the past / 高台過往的影像

*that I watched many times the Uighur dance while listening to the rhythm and melody.*

*It is also here that I got to chat with Sabu Er'jin and his granddaughter Zulai Kezi. Sabu was born in 1950, so is now 72 years old, and his granddaughter is now 30, with two of her own children, ages 8 and 9. His family owns the teahouse restaurant which I visited several times during my stay at Kashgar, now operated by one of his sons and the granddaughter. It may seem strange to many that Sabu has seven grown-up children, in seeming defiance of the two-child policy for minority nationalities, a policy so popularly promoted in the West as one of the narratives about China.*

*Sabu's eldest son has taken on the father's favorite vocation and plays the drum in the Kashi artistic troupe. Second son is manager of a company, third son has a shop in Old Town, while fourth daughter is a security guard, and fifth son is in charge of this teahouse restaurant. The sixth and seventh kids have their own shop and restaurant inside Old Town.*

*Sabu was born and raised in Kashgar. Since a child, he has loved music and has been performing as a drummer for over 50 years. At 32, he joined the Kashi cultural troupe and stayed there for four years before the troupe started touring around China for performance. He travelled to Hangzhou, Suzhou and many other places, performing for five or six years.*

*His son rented the current restaurant space in 2019 and business was good until the pandemic hit. In 2021 business resumed and now each year they can net a profit of over one million RMB. But this year, because of unstable circumstances, business is down again.*

*At the tea house restaurant, they hired a couple of elders to perform together. Based on Uighur customs, the elders start converging around 10am for tea. They would stick around until two to three in the afternoon. It costs 5 RMB for a pot of black tea and a piece of nang, the pitta bread staple of Xinjiang. Tourist tea costs a lot more per pot; health tea at 22, rose tea 58, fruit brew 38, milk tea 78 RMB. Only male members of families come to tea houses, whereas women stay at home caring for household chores.*

*I spent my last night in Kashgar listening to Sabu's drum playing and his singing. Soon his granddaughter Zulai*

Sabu & granddaughter Zulai / 薩布和孫女萊克茲

caught him by his arm and began dancing with him. They danced together for a long time, as the music came from Zulai's mobile phone connected to an amplifier/speaker. Their joyous mood was more telling than words can express, especially contradicting those from foreign accounts.

Now I am on my last stretch of this expedition, set to exit southern Xinjiang and enter western Tibet after a tour of exactly one month within the autonomous region. The road will take our team at least three days of driving over dizzying heights with four mountain passes that exceed 5000 meters in elevation. The weather could change within the same day from sunshine and hot to snow and bitter cold.

The climate likewise has been changing in Xinjiang as its historical and political fortune has shifted over the years. Taking its veil off for now may only reveal in part what may befall it in the future. But as someone who has put in almost half a century of exploration in Asia, in particular in China, I am certain to return, and soon. If not in a car, then on my flying carpet.

Soon too, following my steps into Kashgar will be Michelle Bachelet, High Commissioner of the UN Human Rights Commission. Strange that some 200 human rights groups around the world should try to stop her from visiting Xinjiang; groups I would call "choreographed human rights chorus." For some reason, I have far more respect for groups working on children's rights, women's rights, even animal rights, as they tend to need no veil behind political agenda.

It brought back to mind one American scholar and expert on Xinjiang (then called Sinkiang) *whom I greatly admire; Owen Lattimore. Among his many scholarly works are two books that cover Xinjiang; Pivot of Asia, published in 1950, and Inner Asian Frontiers of China. Others may prefer to call it "Tinder Box of China." Another of his books, also published in 1950, is Ordeal by Slander, the first great book to challenge the McCarthyism then running rampant in America, when Lattimore's reputation for integrity was destroyed by misinformation and lies. Today with the internet, its more the norm than exception.*

*Having gained my journalism degree and lived in the USA for some twenty years, another memory suddenly came back to mind. Between 1969 and 1973, I was Foreign Students Association President at the University of Wisconsin at River Falls. I had the occasion of meeting with some Native Americans who, as a very small group on campus, often banded together with us, feeling a bit foreign like us students from abroad.*

*It was a Chippawa girl from Hayward Wisconsin who introduced me to the book Bury My Heart at Wounded Knee. That should be required reading, Class 101, for those "human rightists" using misinformation to target selective "others." As for honest human rights activists who are striving to right the wrongs of the world through persuasion and active engagement, they are admirable, like Owen Lattimore. Hopefully, Michelle Bachelet will take a higher view, as if flying a magic carpet, too.*

# 飛天魔毯，帶我重返往日時光

我找到一張飛天魔毯，帶我穿越時空，重返二十年前，跨越嶄新的千禧年，再飛回九〇年代、八〇年代，甚至飛往更久遠的七〇年代末期，正是我第一次訪問新疆時。

那時，阿杜瓦哈 (Abdul Wahab) 還沒出生呢，但眼前的阿杜，今年已是三十六歲的青壯年，閃閃發亮的光頭，下巴蓄著稀疏鬍渣，讓他看起來比實際年齡老得多。他身型瘦高，典型維吾爾族與土耳其人的五官外貌，加上偶爾脫口而出的英文，很容易被誤認為外國人。事實上，阿杜是喀什 (Kashi) 老城區一間名氣最高、品質最優的地毯店老闆。當然，今天的喀什最為人津津樂道的，是它在名留歷史的絲綢之路上，成為這段中亞旅途的叉路口。

阿杜從童年開始，便在耳濡目染下被培育成一個熱愛地毯的人。他的父親在大約四十年前開始從事地毯生意，父親到鄉下選購老舊地毯，帶回來清洗後，老毯翻新，再轉手賣給外國遊客。父親的生意剛好跟上中國對西方世界開放的步伐，一時之間，遊客如織，地毯店也門庭若市。二〇〇〇年前後，父親把地毯店搬到喀什老城。當時，十幾歲的阿杜已開始在店裡當父親的幫手，跟在父親身邊學習經營地毯事業。

他們家的地毯生意越做越好，有口皆碑，不僅打響了名號，事業也蒸蒸日上，還紅紅火火到國外，甚至賣到歐洲與美洲等地。後來，他的父親認識了一位巴基斯坦商人，由此而開始從巴基斯坦與阿富汗進口地毯。這些百分之百純羊毛或駱駝毛的地毯，不僅純手工，而且色澤豐富，設計的圖案也編織得比當地地毯還要細緻講究。

到二〇〇六年前，阿杜信心滿滿，決定在北京最熱門的酒吧文化發源區三里屯 (Sanlitun) 開店。一直到二〇一六年娶了來自桂林的妻子後，阿杜又把這家很賺錢的店面收起來，返回老家，加入父親的生意，父子聯手經營。二〇二一年，阿杜的父親因心臟病離世，他和妻子也分道揚鑣，各走各的路。

今天，阿杜的地毯貨源來自多國，包括阿富汗、烏茲別克（以刺繡編織為主）、土庫曼、印度的克什米爾、伊朗、巴基斯坦甚至埃及。還有一些比較特殊少見的地毯出自新疆的和田 (Hotan)。這些從國外進口的地毯，一般會先集中到巴基斯坦，然後再透過物流公司運送，先送抵新疆帕米爾的塔什庫爾干 (Taxkorgan)，最後才送到喀什 (Kashgar) 市。不過，自二〇二〇年新冠疫情爆發後，因為邊界的出入境全面關閉，阿杜的貨源供應也被迫中斷。

最初，大約從二〇〇一至二〇〇五年間，阿杜的父親會親自到巴基斯坦驗貨、收購運送且同步敲定下一批訂單。買賣雙方的誠信逐步建立起來，巴基斯坦地毯商每年都會在五月至十月之間到喀

Images of Gaotai in the past /
高台過往的影像

什來接單，而後續的大部分地毯，則選定阿富汗為主要生產地——原因很多，其中包括勞動成本相對低廉、原物料供應充足且品質更優。到隔年的四月或五月，國外的地毯訂單通常到這時候已滿單，可以準備運送到喀什，然後再送往中國或海外客戶手中。

生意圓圓滿滿時，光是他們這家店的地毯成本價，就多達四十至五十萬人民幣，當然這也表示他們的利潤是相當可觀的。今天，雖然銷量不若以往，市場也萎縮不少，但阿杜仍能維持每年至少一百萬人民幣的盈收，有時候甚至超出一百萬。阿杜的許多客戶對地毯瞭若指掌，而且非常挑剔。因為近期的疫情與出入境的諸多限制，他目前的主要客戶，大多來自中國內地。每一次當觀光團一抵達，阿杜都要給導遊抽成，這筆福利可以讓阿杜留住一群頂端的觀光團，讓他們以阿杜的地毯店為旅遊行程的最後一站。

到目前為止，在這兩層樓的店鋪內，標價最高的地毯是來自新疆和田的編織地毯，每平方公尺有高達五百至六百段編織織目，叫價二十五萬人民幣。另一張由桑蠶絲編織、尺寸較小的和田地毯，和另一張七十年古董級的土庫曼地毯價格一樣，都超過十萬人民幣。桑蠶絲的原料取得，難度越來越高，每平方公尺一千兩百段編織織目，幾乎相當於一千兩百道針目，人力成本高，價格自然也居高不下。

我問阿杜，他會如何挑選一張地毯送給最好的朋友，他不假思索回應：「當然是產自新疆的地毯，因為我是新疆人嘛。」於是，我們買了一些地毯，

Orchestra modern rug / 地毯上現代的樂團

其中有些要送給多年來支持與協助我們的朋友。

當我起身準備離開時,隨口向阿杜提及我最喜歡的喀什區聚落——高台,那是一個距離老城區大約二十分鐘腳程、名副其實位於「高台」上的社區。雖然老城區名聞天下,但不遠處的高台卻鮮為人知;事實上,這塊古老飛地的居民已在當地生活了好幾個世紀。「我小時候常去高台,也常和朋友到那邊閒逛,但現在好久沒去了。」阿杜說完,再補充道:「政府已將所有居民遷離那地方,打算把高台打造成另一個旅遊景點。」

多年前,我曾在獨特的高台社區採訪拍照,那些難忘的往日記憶與舊時光,倏忽湧上心頭,歷歷在目。很可惜,那些古老的泥磚黏土蓋的木頭房屋因為沒有自來水、廁所與基本的管線配置,而不符現在家庭的生活與使用。當然,看在我們這些來自四面八方的外來旅人,這樣的地方獨樹一幟又古色古香,但住在當地的年輕人則不以為然,他們渴望更現代化的生活方式。

我只能乘上我的魔法地毯,一併把萬千思緒載回過去,重溫舊夢。或許,我還可以快速倒帶,重訪許多烙印在腦海、儲存在電腦裡

Images of Gaotai in the past / 高台過往的影像

的影像。這讓我重新意識到我們的紀錄工作多麼任重道遠，留下許多逐漸模糊或消失無蹤的人事物；讓往事不如煙，也讓我們的檔案與展覽重現歷史與榮耀。

阿杜地毯店的隔壁，是樂器行，販售許多不同類型的庫木孜 (kumuzi)，那是一種類似吉他的樂器，有個細長的木柄，與不大的共鳴箱。店內還可見許多大小不一的手鼓，大部分手鼓都配有蟒蛇皮的鼓頭，據說這樣的設計可以發出最優質的樂聲。

再往下走去，是老城區的廣場一角，商店林立，不少賣點心和古董古玩的店家都匯聚於此。其中一間兩邊各有階梯，通往對外延伸的陽台，陽台設計仿若小小劇院，後方開了間庭園式餐廳。陽台上擺了兩張小桌，讓過路旅客可以坐下休息，觀賞廣場風景，同時欣賞兩三位當地音樂工作者的演出。那是我最愛的角落，就位坐下後，一邊小酌啤酒，一邊聆聽鼓聲與庫木孜的樂音裊裊。凡新疆維吾爾族所在之處，無論何處，只要聽到鼓聲，他們的自然回應便是手舞足蹈，聞聲舞動。可以想見，我在這裡已多次一邊聆聽旋律、一邊欣賞維吾爾族翩然起舞。

我就是在這樣的歌舞場合裡，與薩布爾金 (Sabu Er'jin) 與他的孫女祖萊克茲 (Zulai Kezi) 談起話來。薩布出生於一九五〇年，今年七十二歲，而三十歲的孫女祖萊，也已經有自己的兩個孩子，分別是八歲與九歲。薩布家族有自己的茶館餐廳，我在喀什區時，經常光顧他們家的茶館，這家餐廳目前由他的其中一個兒子與孫女經營。薩布有七個孩子，可謂兒孫滿堂，這對許多外人，尤其自以為熟知中國的西方世界專家來說，似乎有違他們對中國的想像，但事實上，中國不僅對少數民族從未實施二胎化政策，甚至鼓勵他們多生。

薩布的大兒子承接父親最愛的工作——在喀什藝術團擔任鼓手。老二在一家公司擔任經理職，老三在老城區自己開店做生意，老四是女兒，目前當警衛，老五則負責經營這家茶館餐廳。第六個孩子與老么都在老城區有自己的店面與餐館，各有事業。

薩布是道地的喀什人，生於此、長於此。他從小就熱愛音樂，當了超過五十年的鼓手。三十二歲那年，他參加喀什文工團，在這個藝術團隊開始巡迴中國各地演出前，他一待就是四年。薩布跟著團隊遊走各地，包括杭州、蘇州等地，全心投身這段擊鼓演出將近五、六年時間。

薩布的兒子在二〇一九年租下目前的這家餐廳，在新冠疫情爆發前，餐廳生意一直都很好。熬過疫情考驗，從二〇二一年開始逐漸恢復過去榮景，目前，每年的淨獲利都超過一百萬人民幣。但今年卻因外在環境不穩定，而再度影響餐館生意。

薩布家的茶餐廳聘請了幾位長者來表演。依照維吾爾族傳統習俗，長輩喜歡在上午十點開始陸續在茶館相聚，一起喝茶聊天。一壺紅茶，外加一塊類似胡餅的新疆主食「饢」，簡單的點心茶飲收費約五元人民幣；當大夥兒把話匣子一開，經常一待就到下午兩三點才會各自散去。觀光旅遊的一壺熱茶，價格普遍較高——保健茶二十二元、玫瑰茶五十八元、水果茶三十八元、奶茶最高，一壺要七十八元。一般而言，只有家中的男性成員才會到茶館來消費談話，打發時間，而女性則留守家中，操持家務。

我在喀什的最後一晚，是聽著薩布充滿節奏的鼓聲與歌聲渡過的。不久，他的孫女祖萊湊過來拉起他的手臂，開始邀請祖父起身共舞，只見祖孫倆載歌載舞，矯若遊龍。他們跟著祖萊從手機連接播放器的音樂，跳得開眉展眼，彷彿地久天長般不捨停步，喜形於色又溢於言表；此情此景，與外界對新疆的繪聲繪影與帶目的性報導，迥然有別。

我現在正處於這趟探索之旅的最後一段路，在這片自治區內完成扎扎實實一個月的考察後，我準備離開新疆南部，動身前往西藏西部。這段迢迢遠路至少要花三天時間才能抵達目的地，途中還會經過令人暈頭轉向的崎嶇山路，總計是四座超過五千公尺的高海拔山口。這些地方的天候陰晴不定，一天內可能從陽光普照到風霜雪雨，善變幅度之巨，完全難以捉摸。

事實上，新疆的歷史與近年來的政治命途，也與起伏劇烈的氣候一樣，詭譎多變。在當下情境揭開其面紗，恐怕只能突顯未來可能發生的事。不過，以一個在亞洲探索近半世紀，尤其在中國「行之」

Teahouse/restaurant at square / 廣場上的茶館和餐廳

Sabu's Uighur orchestra / 薩布的維吾爾族樂隊

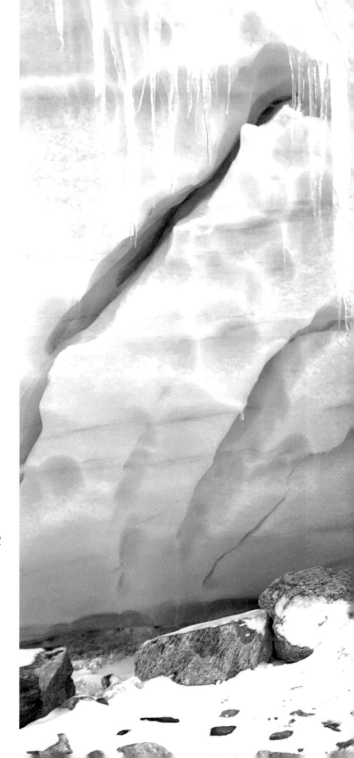

慕
士
塔
格
峰

# MUZTAGH ATA

on the slopes of Muztagh Ata, Xinjiang – May 2022

## MUZTAGH ATA
### A 7509 meters peak in the Pamirs

In Uighur language, Muztagh Ata means father of ice mountains. Looking from afar or close-up, one can understand how the name came about. It is a huge mound of ice and snow from foothill to the top, not a pinnacle peak but a dome-like one, reaching up to just over 7500 meters, with many gigantic cracks and ice valleys taken up by perpetual glacier formation. In all there are 16 glaciers, with the largest one running over 21 kilometers in length.

The mountain sits squarely on a large base beside the ancient Silk Road that exits China into the Indian subcontinent or, through the Wakhan Corridor, into Afghanistan. And so, since historical times, trade caravans, religious pilgrims or political emissaries would pass right by it heading in or out of China. Its grandiosity must have captured the imagination of travelers over several millennia.

Before the founding of the PRC, several attempts were made to climb it; by famed explorer Sven Hedin at the turn of the century, by archaeologist Aurel Stein, and not the least, in 1947, by Eric Shipton, one of the icons of early Himalayan climbing, who was then serving as Consul for the British at Kashgar. Shipton almost made it to the top but was turned back due to extreme snowfall.

It seems natural that when China opened its border to foreign climbers, this was among the very first mountains for which climbers sought permits for attempts to reach its summit. So it was in 1980 that my friend Ned Gillette managed to organize a climbing team to scale it. In his team were two other famous climbers, Jan Reynolds and Galen Rowell. Ned and I met at the National Geographic, as we both explored and wrote for the magazine.

Ned's team not only reached the summit but descended on skis at night in what Ned said was "perfect powder" snow, "like skiing into the bowels of the earth", downhill over a 1500 meters loss of elevation. This became the highest ski descent of a mountain on record. Over the subsequent years, he bagged several other "Firsts" as trophies, but he also came back again to the Silk Road in 1993. Ned seemed to have caught not only the bug for adventure, but also for exploration.

With his wife and a Moroccan boy, they used a camel caravan to go from China all the way to the Mediterranean Sea, somewhat reversing the journey of Marco Polo. Before this 10,000-kilometer journey, he came to stay at my mountain home in the Angeles National Forest behind Pasadena in order to use my library of exploration accounts to work out his logistics. His intent was also to use satellite links to make intermittent educational broadcast to schools in the US while undertaking his long expedition.

I was sad to hear of Ned's death at the age of 53, in 1998, while he was on yet another expedition, just across the border on the other side of the Karakoram Mountains near the disputed border of Kashmir between Pakistan and India. He was shot inside his climbing tent by bandits who intended to rob his wife and him. His wife also sustained major injury from gun shots.

Muztagh Ata circa 1984 / 慕士塔格峰於 1984 年

Camping in snow / 雪地裡紮營

*My own experience with Muztagh Ata was somewhat less dramatic, yet nonetheless memorable, in 1984 and 1993. These two occasions provided my early exposure to the Kirgiz and Tajik nationalities of China. The Kirgiz in particular resided right on the western foothills of the mountain. I managed to set camp also in the foothills among them. It became the cover photo of my book From Machuria to Tibet.*

*Almost thirty years after my last visit, the situation has changed drastically for this current expedition. The road is now fully paved. The Pamirs had become a tourist destination before the pandemic hit, and Muztagh Ata was a must-see stop, or what is now called a "punch card" spot, for sending selfies home.*

*Glacier Number Four, one of the easier glaciers to approach, is now advertised as a highlight for visitors to the Pamirs. A 15-kilometer dirt road beyond a grand gate leads up to a parking area at 4511 meters elevation. Another forty-five minutes hike up two hundred meters higher in elevation would take one to the tongue of the glacier.*

*But that's all speculation; projections by the few people allowed into the "park" so far. The plan is to open up access to this glacier in due course, but not yet. A year ago, some visitors managed to sneak in, illegally, and an accident occurred. Now the entire glacier is closed.*

*Not taking "no" as an answer has always been one of the tenets of my explorer's motto. So, through a friend who is a big time real estate developer in Kashi (Kashgar), we were quickly connected to management of this Number Four Glacier Park. We were told that on the morning of my intended* visit, a caretaker would be waiting at the gate for our arrival.

Following a night camping at a cool 3650 meters in Subashi Kirgiz village by Lake Karakul, we drove along the western foothill of Muztagh Ata. When we went to bed after 9 pm, the sky was clear and still lit at this westernmost part of China. But by morning when I woke up, all our cars and tents were covered with a thin veil of snow. Higher up the mountain, heavier snow-covered hilltops, with a gradually thinner coat of it descending down the mountains; most beautiful scenery as backdrop to my breakfast and coffee we prepared at camp.

We reached the gate of the glacier park at 10 am. A Kirgiz gatekeeper was waiting and waved us through. No questions asked as if all were scripted and understood. I could see a large modern structure, almost complete, that will become the future entrance and visitor's center for the park. Park management had notified us earlier that

Yak in snow / 雪地裡的犛牛

Book Cover / 書封

we were not only allowed onto the glacier, but could camp there as we pleased. Having the right connections certainly helped, as anywhere in the world.

Fifteen kilometers on a dirt road with some easy climbing, we could see several glaciers in the distant, as well as a few closer ones. There were also small herds of yaks grazing in some faraway hills. Finally, we could see a huge glacier in front of us as the road ended in a large parking area at the trail head to reach the Number Four Glacier. Here the elevation was 4,300 meters above sea level.

The hike to the side of the glacier tongue took about 45 minutes as it was around two kilometers away, and some 200 meters higher in elevation. When I reached the glacier tongue, my altimeter registered 4524 meters. Some of our team members were very excited as this was their first adventure so close to a glacier, its icefield and an ice lake.

I had my glacier goggles on as I took my slow steps to reach the glacier. I used these same shades when I first went to the Yangtze source in 1985, and then again in 1995 and 2005. Visiting another glacier reminded me of the several glacier sources I have put my feet on. Back then, getting to a glacier required intrepid exploration for scientists or explorers, at times riding horses for days to reach them. Today, our younger generation can literally drive up to such remote destinations.

While my friend Ned was the first American to summit Muztagh Ata in 1980, today a climbing outfitter offers a ski expedition to Muztagh Ata to the tune of 6,690 USD per person, less than a *dollar for each meter of elevation of the mountain. And that is only a fraction of the high five-figure charges for an average Everest summit attempt.*

*As for myself, I am quite happy to enjoy my moment of tranquility sitting under one of the ice caves in the bowel of Number Four Glacier of the Father of Ice Mountains, savoring the taste of an icicle from above my head. It is surely a different age now, for the mountain, and for myself as well, having explored China's remotest regions for almost half a century. I must now retrace my steps back to my camper van, as my hot latte is waiting.*

*Clouds are fast coming in and snow has started drifting. While much of the world is seeing the effect of climate change with another hot summer, we here on the high Pamirs can no doubt expect another night of camping out in the snow.*

Icicle at glacier / 冰河的冰柱

Altimeter reading / 高度計數字

Glacier close-up / 冰河近照

# 慕士塔格峰

帕米爾高原上的 7509 公尺高山

維吾爾語的慕士塔格峰 (Muztagh Ata)，帶有「冰山之父」的意思。無論遠觀或近看，「冰山」之由來，實至名歸。這座大山，從山腳到山頂都被冰雪堆積，有別於一般尖頂的高峰，慕士塔格峰的山巔呈半球圓頂，高達 7500 公尺，山峰結構有許多巨大裂縫與冰谷，形成永久的冰川；其中十六條冰川中，最長的超過二十一公里。

遠古時期要經過絲綢之路時，無論你從中國出發前往印度，或穿越中國與阿富汗接壤的「瓦罕走廊」(Wakhan Corridor) 進入阿富汗，總要和這座高聳入雲的慕士塔格峰打照面，她像個巨無霸基地，端端正正坐立於絲綢之路旁。因此，從古至今，無論貿易商旅、宗教朝聖信徒或政治密使，若要進出中國，這是必經之路。數千年以來，慕士塔格峰的雄偉壯觀，備受矚目，不知激發多少旅人的想像。

在中華人民共和國成立以前，曾有爬山隊伍嘗試攀登慕士塔格峰的幾次紀錄——在世紀交替期間，著名探險家斯文・赫定 (Sven Hedin)、考古學家奧萊爾・斯坦因 (Aurel Stein) 與早期攀登喜馬拉雅山其中一位指標性代表人物艾瑞克・西普頓 (Eric Shipton)——都曾親臨這座高峰；值得一提的是，西普頓當時受派到喀什區擔任英國領事，他幾乎登頂成功，但最終因嚴重降雪而撤退。

Muztagh Ata 2022 / 士塔格峰於 2022 年

自中國對國外登山者開放邊界以來，登上慕士塔格峰，幾乎已成為登山者摩拳擦掌、最熱衷申請許可證的首選山峰之一。我認識的幾位朋友也對此躍躍欲試，於是，一九八〇年，我的友人奈德‧吉列特 (Ned Gillette) 籌組了一支登山隊，準備攀登慕士塔格峰。團隊裡還有另兩位著名登山家——簡‧雷諾斯 (Jan Reynolds) 和加倫‧羅威爾 (Galen Rowell)。奈德和我因曾經為《國家地理雜誌》進行荒野探索與報導而相識。

奈德的登山團隊不僅登頂成功，而且在夜裡的雪地上滑雪而下，奈德形容當下情境為一場完美的「粉末」登場，「仿若滑向地球深處」，下山的海拔高度超過一千五百米，陡降高度驚人，而創下有史以來最高的「滑雪下山」紀錄。隨後幾年內，奈德把親身體驗的好些「第一」當成戰利品，並在一九九三年重返絲綢之路。看來，這位荒野登山大師不僅對冒險樂此不疲，也開始愛上各種探索活動。

奈德與妻子，以及一位摩洛哥男孩，一起隨著駱駝隊從中國出發，一路行進至地中海，和當年馬可波羅的長途之旅剛好「反其道而行」。奈德踏上這段一萬公里的旅途之前，他先來找我，我當時還住在美國加州帕莎蒂娜 (Pasadena) 後方的洛杉磯國家森林的山間木屋；他想要使用我的探索圖書資料庫，來解決他後勤補給的需求。奈德也想利用衛星連結，把他漫長的荒野探險，作為不定期的教育素材，提供美國的教育單位，廣為流傳。

但世事難料，一九九八年聽聞奈德離世的新聞時，我感到無比遺憾難過。他當時才五十三歲，正值壯年，卻在另一趟探索旅途中遇害——地點就在巴基斯坦與印度之間、靠近喀喇崑崙山脈附近一個充滿邊境爭議的克什米爾邊界。持槍歹徒從奈德和妻子的登山帳篷外發出行劫，奈德被槍殺，妻子則受重傷。

Glacier as storm approaches / 暴風雪接近冰河

我在一九八四與一九九三年曾經兩度前往慕士塔格峰，雖然沒那麼戲劇性，卻也難忘。那是我最早接觸中國柯爾克孜族與塔吉克族的經歷。尤其是聚居於慕士塔格峰西麓的柯爾克孜族，我還記得自己就在那山腳下紮營，住在他們當中，當時留下的印象，格外深刻。

這回舊地重遊，離上一次已將近三十年，時過境遷，滄海桑田，此番探索已和上一次迥然有別，差異極大。道路全面鋪上瀝青柏油，在未受新冠疫情衝擊前，帕米爾高原已搖身一變為旅遊區，慕士塔格峰也成了必遊的觀光景點，套句現代白話文是「打卡熱點」，在高山前自拍一張，立刻傳送回家。

相對而言，四號冰川是慕士塔格峰較容易親近的冰川之一，現在也被大肆宣傳，成了帕米爾高原上的旅遊亮點。先越過一座宏偉大門，踏上一段十五公里長的土路，一直前行至海拔 4511 公尺的停車場。下車後再往上步行一段歷時 45 分鐘的兩百公尺山路，便能抵達長窄條狀的冰舌。

當然，以上這些說明與數據，都只是理論上的預估；也是迄今為止獲准進入「公園」內少數人的預測。這段進入冰川入口的路線規劃還在研擬階段，目前仍未開放。曾經有遊客在一年前試圖非法闖入，還發生了意外；現在整個冰川區域已封閉起來，不對外開放。

從不把「不」當答案——這是身為探險工作者的我，奉行不變的座右銘。於是，透過一位在喀什區從事房地產開發的朋友協助，我很快便與「四號冰川公園」的管理層取得聯繫。不久，好消息傳來，我們獲知在預定訪視的當日早上，會安排一位看守人員在門口等我們。

我們當時還在 3650 公尺的高山冰磧湖——喀拉庫勒 (Lake Karakul) 湖邊的吉爾吉斯蘇巴什村——紮營

Glacier from above / 俯瞰冰河

住了一晚；隔天，我們繞著慕士塔格峰的西麓，驅車下山。晚上九點準備就寢時，抬頭望天，這片中國最西邊的天空仍清淨明亮。隔日清晨醒來時，我們所有的車子和帳篷都覆蓋了一層薄雪。可想而知，越往高處走，山頂越是冰凝雪積，而逐漸稀薄的雪層則順著山勢而下移；那天在營區準備早餐與咖啡時，我們背後的天然佈景美得令人屏息靜氣。

上午十點左右，我們抵達冰川公園大門。一位柯爾克孜族守門員已在那裡等候，對我們揮手示意，讓我們入內。沒有任何提問，也無須多言，彷彿一切早已安排妥當，各得其所。聳立眼前的，是一座幾乎完工的大型現代化建築，顯然就是未來的公園入口處與遊客中心。公園的管理人員已經預先告知，准我們自由進入冰川區域，還可以在那裡隨意紮營。無論在世界各地，建立合宜的關係，肯定對我們的工作大有助益。

走一段十五公里的上坡土路，眼前近處有冰川，遠方的幾個冰川也清晰可見。山丘上風吹雪低見「犛牛」，低頭吃草。路的盡頭是大型的停車場，那是抵達四號冰川的小路。這裡的海拔高度是 4300 公尺，我們也終於親眼看到橫擺前方的巨大冰川。

總計走了四十五分鐘，才走到冰舌的旁側，這段大約兩公里的路，高度陡然攀升了兩百公尺。當我抵達冰舌時，我的高度計顯示我們的已置身 4524 公尺高峰。團隊裡的一些成員異常興奮，因為那是他們生平第一次如此近距離探索一座冰川、冰原與冰湖。

我戴著冰川護目鏡，「步履薄冰」地緩步走向冰川。我想起一九八五年第一次到長江源頭、一九九五年與二〇〇五年再二度、三度舊地重訪，我都戴同樣這副護目鏡。眼見冰川，腳踏冰川，也使我想起人生中曾經親近過的幾個冰川源頭。那個年代，走近冰川是件不得了的高難度壯舉，是科學家或探險家堅韌無畏的工作，有時還得騎馬好幾天才能抵達目的地，長途顛簸而曲折。今天，我們年輕的這一代，只要開著車子，彷彿沒有到不了的窮途極地。

一九八〇年，我的朋友奈德是第一位成功登上慕士塔格峰的美國人；今天，根據一家戶外登山商家所提供的「慕士塔格峰滑雪探險」的全套體驗活動，每人收費 6690 美元，平均算起來，每登上一公尺高度還不足一美元。這樣的費用和攀登珠穆朗瑪峰「入門款」最起碼的五位數高收費相比，算是經濟實惠。

至於我，能坐在「冰山之父」四號冰川的其中一個雪原冰窟中，享受片刻的寧謐清幽，感受冰柱頂著頭的百般冷滋味，我滿心歡喜。這確實是個徹底不同的世代，對高山是如此，對我這個曾經以半個世紀的時間，千山萬水到過中國最偏遠之地的人來說，這種日新月異的反思，同樣深刻。該是時候回到我的露營車了，我的熱拿鐵已在召喚我。

風雲過眼，一擁而上，雪花開始飄落。當世界多數地區因氣候變遷而又迎來另一個酷暑難耐的夏季時，我們卻在帕米爾高原上期待另一個雪中露營的夜晚。

HM at glacier / HM 於冰河
Drone shot of camp / 無人機拍攝營地

從喀什到拉薩（上集）

# KASHGAR TO LHASA (part 1)

Xinjiang/Tibet – June 2, 2022

## *KASHGAR TO LHASA (part 1)*
### *Muslim to Buddhist enclaves of China*

*The drive east from Kashgar begins along the historical caravan route of the ancient Silk Road. Since over a century ago, during the Qing Dynasty, and throughout the years of the Kuomintang rule of the Republic of China, Kashgar was considered a crossroads of the ancient Silk Road that connected China to Central Asia, the Middle East and Europe – a link from the Oriental to the Occidental world.*

*In fact, Kashgar's importance as a citadel guarding the entrance and exit point of the Chinese empire lasted to the time when the Communist Party took over the entire country in 1949. Kashgar's significance before the founding of the PRC was also demonstrated not only by the stopovers of caravansaries, but also by the establishment of several European consular offices, including those representing the Russian and British Empires. Many major trading companies and missionaries also established their outposts in this far-flung desert oasis that sat next to the Taklimakan, second largest moving desert in the world, its name meaning "going in without coming out" in the Turkic Uighur language.*

*I have had the great good fortune of visiting Kashgar, known today as Kashi, and the edges of that*

Uighur desert family 1993 / 沙漠裡維吾爾家族於 1993 年　　Desert edge Uighur 1993 / 沙漠邊界維吾爾族於 1993 年

*desert several times; in the late 1970s and throughout the 1980s and 1990s, up to the present. We conducted wildlife, archaeological, ethnographic and even religious studies in the region. My book Islamic Frontiers of China recounted some of those studies.*

*Back during the epoch of the Tang Dynasty, from the 5th to 10th Century, this region of western China embraced Buddhism, which had spread from India to the Middle Kingdom. It wasn't until a few centuries later that Islam began to sprout, and then set roots, in Xinjiang. We stopped at one of the ruins of early Buddhist sites, barely thirty kilometers southeast of Kashgar.*

*Mo'er-si was one of the earliest Buddhist monasteries in China, dating back to the Third Century, some 1800 years ago. It was abandoned over a thousand years ago due to climate change and rivers drying up. In 2001, the site was inscribed as a national level cultural heritage site. Wang Binghua, an old friend who recently retired from*

Excavated sculpted face / 出土的人臉雕像

a long-time appointment as Director of the Institute of Archaeology in Xinjiang, recommended that I stop for a visit there.

Several early explorers stopped at Mo'er-si and did some basic mapping and excavation, which yielded few objects of significance. Among them were the British-Hungarian Silk Road archaeologist Aurel Stein, followed shortly later by French Archaeologist Paul Pelliot. Both later became famous, or notorious, as they removed large amounts of artifacts and sutras from the Dunhuang Caves. Pelliot, after excavation at Mo'er-si, passed it off as a site with little value.

However, for today's historians, Mo'er-si has come to show something that, while not necessarily of archaeological value, illustrates that the region's people, predominantly of Uighur descent, were originally Buddhists rather than Muslim. Even the Tang Dynasty pilgrim monk Xuan Zang noted the area was a Buddhist base when he passed through in the mid- seventh Century. Such information encourages us to understand that beliefs are not necessarily predestined or permanent but have evolved over time.

Serious and coordinated excavation did not begin until the last few years. Beginning in 2019, a team led by scientists and scholars of the Xinjiang Institute of Archaeology, together with professors and students from the

Nationality University of Beijing, conducted a multi-year survey and excavation of the site. So far, it has resulted in the discovery of over ten thousand pieces of pot shards and artifact fragments at the foot of the two large temple towers and on the adjacent grounds, sites of former dwellings. As we visited the open site, workers had just begun to fence off this important area before the excavation team would start a new season of work in July.

Beyond Mo'er-si, we reached Yarkand (Shache today) two hundred kilometers away, within a couple hours. In the past, a camel caravan would have taken days to skirt around the southern edge of the Taklimakan desert. Today, the main town of the county is Yecheng, an oasis hub from whence going east one could reach the ancient town of Hotan and heading south one would be on the high road to cross into Tibet.

One of the early explorers of the Silk Road was Carl Gustaf Mannerheim. Between 1906 to 1908, Mannerheim, a Fin and an officer within the Czarist Russian army, led a scientific expedition along the Silk Road which ended in Beiping (today's Beijing). His travels are well documented by the photographs, writings and maps about the Xinjiang region of the Silk Road in his massive volume Across Asia. It was published in 1940, by which time Mannerheim had led an army to successfully establish the independence of Finland during the First World War. By the end of the Second World War, Mannerheim had become the president of Finland.

I have studied and followed the Asiatic expedition work of Mannerheim and have written an article about him and visited his home, now made into a museum, in Helsinki. I have even visited a courtyard park with his statue in Montreux Switzerland where he spent his last days. His early work in western China is less well known, but nonetheless important. Perhaps his description of Yarkand and its people are of relevance in recounting sentiments even of the educated class from over a century ago, as Mannerheim is an early explorer to China that I *hold in high esteem.*

*On page 47 of his monumental work, Mannerheim described the "sart" people, a term the Russians commonly used at the time for Uighurs of western China, as "lazy, and content to live for the passing hour, from hand to mouth. If he earns something to-day, he will do no more so long as the money lasts. During the melon season, in particular, his inclination to do nothing is at its height. He enjoys the excellent juicy fruit and sings and plays far into the night.... Bazaar gossip, however, is so developed that news spreads like wildfire from town to town, if not as rapidly as by telegraph, at any rate as surely."*

*Such a narrative of the local people would be deemed politically insensitive today. Much of it is almost unfit for recounting in this day and age. Ironically, many from the West today seem to consider the same people to be incapable of doing wrong, and vehemently defend them against any criticism. Perhaps it fits a predetermined narrative and portrayal of the government of China as oppressor.*

*Mannerheim's ending paragraph on Yarkand, in page 61, is also quite telling, indicative of conditions in the past. "Venereal diseases are far and away the most prevalent. Owing to faulty treatment, or rather the want of any kind of treatment, they occur in a very severe form. Among infectious diseases smallpox and typhus are common, especially the former. But the population seldom applies for treatment. A deformity that is so widespread here that it can scarcely be called an illness, but rather a normal occurrence, is*

Yarkand mosque 2022 / 葉爾羌清真寺於 2022 年

goitre. It develops the most astonishing size and forms. It is ascribed to the influence of the water and nothing is done to obviate this. It is a joke among the people of Yarkand that you cannot be a true Yarkandlik unless you possess a respectable goitre." Such pictures also graced the pages of Mannerheim's book.

Today the people of Yarkand, or Yecheng as it is now known, appear to be in much better health. However, the city seems a bit more tense than Kashgar, reflecting the fact that there were organized extremist activities there some years ago. Nonetheless, it is more relaxed than in 2018 when I last visited.

In a museum on the edge of town, there is an exhibit about the China-India military skirmishes of 1962. Soon we would again be at that hot spot before crossing into Tibet, so we made a quick visit to the museum, which has a retired tank of more current vintage sitting in its courtyard.

As a long-time keen observer of China's contemporary military history, I can pick out small errors even in museum displays. For example, pictures depicting the battlefront had the Beijing 212 Jeep. That model did not begin production until 1965, but here in the museum it was featured as being involved in the 1962 battle. I knew its development history well, as I had visited the jeep factory in Beijing in 1979. Likewise the Liberation Brand trucks featured are likely from a later year's photograph. Nonetheless, it did not diminish the theme and purpose of the exhibit.

Our next leg, on National Highway 219 from Yecheng to Aksai Chin, was almost 600 kilometers and took over sixteen hours of driving. Along the way, we stopped for lunch and to gas up at the small Tajik community of Kekeya. Here we were near the historic caravan route that led up to, or down from, the Chinese Pamirs.

Li Na, our logistics manager, took the opportunity to collect a few more hand-embroidered women's hats for our exhibits, and Tsomo took some more field notes from interviews with the ladies. When Taji Guli, a Tajik lady of 60 years old, knew we were interested in her hand-embroidered hat, she went home and brought out two more newer ones, not knowing that we were far more interested in older specimens, in particular the one she was wearing.

Ziwa Guli, twenty years of age, came from the Fifth Village among the five villages of Kekeya and was working as a part-time waitress/receptionist at the waystation where we stopped for lunch. Her family of five was representative of an average household, with around 300 sheep and 25 yaks. There were 99 households within the five villages with a total of 319 people, averaging around three people to a family. They were all Tajik.

After Kekeya, we crossed a series of four high, snow-bound passes, through snow and hail, to travel from Xinjiang

Museum display of 1962 battle /
博物館展示 1962 年的戰爭

Military equipment display / 展示軍事裝備

Photo display / 照片

Windy road pass / 彎曲道路到隘口
Highest road pass / 隘口最高的道路

to Tibet - most telling of the geographic and cultural transition from low desert land to the highest plateau on earth. From desert plants like poplar and red willow, and animals like sheep and camel, we gradually entered high alpine scrub and yak country. From the Islamic realm of the Tajik and Uighur, we moved into the domain of the Tibetan living a Buddhist life.

Along the way were some of the longest switch-back sections of the road to gain elevation. The grandiose and formidable Karakoram mountains on our right, or to the South, where dominated by K2 at an elevation of 8611 meters. In addition to its record as second highest mountain in the world, it can also claim the second highest death rate in the world of those attempting to summit it. Its challenge to mountaineers is almost unsurpassed. It is reported that around 25% of those attempting to summit it have died. While there may be as many as 500 summitting Everest in any given year, there can be none in a year for K2.

I recalled a feat, one of many, by my close friend Captain Moon Chin who turned 109 earlier this year. In June 1942 during WWII, he took a C-53 (the transport variation of a DC-3) and successfully flew across the Karakoram near K2 from Yarkand in Xinjiang to Peshawar in what was then India, now a part of Pakistan. This was planned as an alternative Western Hump route, in case the Japanese should close off the eastern

*Himalayan Hump if they took all of Burma (Myanmar). The US Air Force tried several times, in a more advanced C-87 but in vain, to cross the Karakoram from India into Xinjiang China before Moon was called up and successfully undertook this seemingly hopeless task.*

*For my own part, I failed again to access the Karakoram Pass, a historical caravan route between this region and Kashmir, just as in the past several attempts I had made when in this vicinity. Once a trading outpost between China, Pakistan and India, this pass is today a military hot spot. I satisfied myself by staying one night at the road junction leading to the border, at a most unusual hostel that had just opened for business - one made from stacks of shipping containers, though we are thousands of kilometers from the ocean.*

Long descent to Tibet / 長途下降往西藏

Also at the junction was a military first-aid clinic. I got myself a free prescription of painkillers from the PLA to harness my constantly ascending tooth ache, which ascends as if in coordination with the rise of altitude. The camouflaged-uniformed medics in charge were both courteous and friendly.

Crossing three high passes at well over 5000 meters elevation, with the Jieshan Daban (Border Mountain Pass) and Hongtu Daban (Red Earth Pass) posted as 5347 meters and 5380 meters respectively, took us to Aksai Chin. I cherished sending home pictures of our team wrapped in down jackets while our friends further south were already entering the summer heat of a fast-warming globe. The area is a huge tract of land with approximately 38,000 square kilometers, roughly the size of Bhutan and a bit larger than Taiwan, all mostly above 5000 meters. It belongs to Hotan of Xinjiang administratively, but geographically it is an extension of the Tibetan plateau. Here is a major point of contention between China and India, though firmly now in the hands and under the control of China.

This flash point hosted a month-long battle between the two countries in 1962, after China, in the late 1950s, constructed a road of strategic importance from Xinjiang into Tibet. The area was formerly wilderness with no defined border, thus a perfect place for political contention leading to military confrontation. The battle ended with China holding the area permanently ever since.

The wildlife of the Tibetan plateau began to show themselves, first in scattered locations and small numbers, then more and more, and ultimately even in herds. There were Wild Ass, Tibetan Antelope, and an occasional Tibetan Gazelle. Once we ran into a large herd of female Tibetan

Antelope, numbering a good couple hundred, perhaps beginning their long migration for the hidden calving ground where they will begin giving birth to young lambs between mid-June and early July.

I feel some consolation that many of these animals now roam right up to the road, oblivious to us passers-by. This illustrates that the conservation efforts by the government are bearing fruit, after long years of awareness-building and education, coupled with the threat of strict penalties if animals are poached. My team was surprised to see that even when our drone was sent up to film them, the Tibetan Antelope stayed put and continued to graze even while the drone was closing in overhead.

After three full days of driving out from Kashgar, a high monumental gate spanning the road overhead proclaimed that we were finally and safely entering Tibet. We had covered a distance that would have taken a month of caravan travel a century ago. From here to Lhasa would be another three to four days for us, or another month for a caravan.

Our mode of travels have become much more efficient, but I fear that our breadth and depth of experience has become shallower. By reading books from the past, I can now fill the gaps and appreciate an era when time was slow and distances far.

Border into Tibet / 進入西藏的邊境

# 從喀什到拉薩（上集）穆斯林走進中國佛家的飛地

從喀什往東行駛，我們沿著歷史上商旅隊頻繁往來的古絲綢之路，開展我們這段長途跋涉。一個世紀以前的清朝，以及整段中華民國國民黨統治時期，喀什就被認定為古絲綢之路的一個叉路口，這個連接起中國與中亞、中東和歐洲大陸的關鍵路口，是跨越東西方世界的主要橋樑。

事實上，喀什扮演的角色，在共產黨一九四九年全面掌管整個國家前，一直是個守護邊界的重要關閘與要塞。在中華人民共和國成立以前，不只長途往返的商旅隊會駐足停留於此，許多歐洲國家也以喀什為據點，建立他們的辦事處，包括代表俄羅斯與英帝國的領事機構。此外，還有許多主要的貿易公司與傳教士組織，也紛紛在這遙遠的沙漠綠洲成立他們的基地。緊鄰喀什的沙漠，是世界第二大流動式沙漠塔克拉瑪干 (Taklimakan)，在突厥維吾爾語裡，這名稱的原意是「有進無出」。

從七〇年代末期，一直到八〇、九〇年代，再到此時當下，能多次進出這塊土地，深入喀什與沙漠邊緣；我深感榮幸。我們在這地區進行了野生動物觀察、考古紀錄、人種誌甚至宗教研究；我在英國出版的著作《中國的伊斯蘭邊境》(Islamic Frontiers of China) 也曾紀錄其中一些研究內容與論述。

回溯古老的喀什，其實，早在五至十世紀的唐朝時期便已找到相關記載，這片中國的西域之地，最初先是接受了從印度傳到中原的佛教。佛教在喀什深耕了幾世紀以後，伊斯蘭教才開始在新疆萌芽，並逐漸紮根成長。我們在喀什東南方不到三十公里處發現了早期的佛教遺址。

Mo er-si Buddhist tower / 莫爾寺佛塔

位於喀什區的莫爾寺，是中國最早期的佛教寺廟之一，寺廟歷史可追溯到第三世紀，大約一千八百年前。因為氣候變遷與河床乾枯，莫爾寺在一千多年前即被棄置；二〇〇一年時，這片遺址被列為國家一級重點文物保護單位。我的老朋友王炳華，從新疆文物考古研究所的所長職位退休，他建議我到當地停留參觀。

早期曾有慕名而來的探險家，為莫爾寺進行一些基本測繪與挖掘等工作，但沒有發現任何具有考究意義的文物；參與這項考古計畫的探險家，包括英國的匈牙利籍絲綢之路的專家奧里爾·斯坦因 (Aurel Stein)，隨後跟上考察研究的，還有法國考古學家保羅·伯希和 (Paul Pel-liot)。這兩位大師後來都因從敦煌石窟取出大量文物與佛經而舉世聞名，但此「聞名」也或許會被視為惡名昭彰，就看你從什麼角度來檢視這件事了。伯希和在莫爾寺完成挖掘工作後，把這座古老寺廟視為沒啥價值的遺址，而放棄追究。

不過，今天的歷史學家則不以為然，他們認為，即時莫爾寺所展示的文物不一定具備考古收藏價值，但這座寺廟的存在是最佳的明證——喀什區的族群，尤其最主要的維吾爾族後裔，他們的祖先是佛教徒，而非穆斯林。就連唐朝的玄奘大師在七世紀中葉取經行經當地時，也曾留意到喀什區確實是個佛教基地。這些資訊有助於我們理解一個事實：原來所謂宗教信仰，未必是早已注定的天命或恆常不變的道理，它是歷經日積月累的推移與演變而來。

一直等到最近幾年，有關莫爾寺的挖掘與考古工作，才以嚴謹與調度各方的考察法，正式啟動。二〇一九年開始，由新疆文物考古研究所的科學家與學者所主導的研究團隊，與北京民族大學的教授與學生，聯手對莫爾寺遺址展開多年的考察與挖掘。到目前為止，這群研究團隊已在廟宇的兩座塔樓下與鄰近的地面，發現一萬多塊鍋壺碎片和文物殘餘，這些區域應是過去的住宅遺址，才會找到這些民生物品。當我們繼續參觀這個未正式開放遺址時，工人剛剛開始把重要文物出土的地方，以柵欄圍起來，保留原址原狀，等候挖掘團隊在七月展開新一季的工作。

過了莫爾寺，我們在幾個小時內，抵達兩百公里以外的葉爾羌 (Yarkand)——今天稱之為莎車縣的地方。相較過去，駱駝隊需要耗費好幾天時間才能繞過這片塔克拉瑪干沙漠

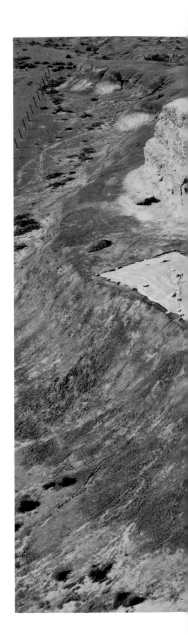

Mo er-si with excavation site covered / 莫爾寺挖掘場址被覆蓋

重。此外，天花與斑疹傷寒也是當地普遍流行的傳染病，其中尤以天花最常見。然而，當地病患很少尋求醫療救助。另外，甲狀腺腫大到幾乎變形，也是另一種『普遍化』到見怪不怪的常態狀況，腫脹的程度與型態相當驚人。當地人把這問題歸咎於有問題的飲用水，但也只能束手無策，無從改善與解決。一如葉爾羌這裡流行的笑話，你若還沒得過可敬可佩的甲狀腺疾病，就不算是個真正的葉爾羌人。」曼納海姆把這些與疾病相關的敘述附上照片，說明與紀錄於他的書中。

今天，葉爾羌人，或我們現在稱之為葉城的居民，他們的健康狀況已漸入佳境。不過，由於這幾年陸續出現一些有組織的極端主義活動，這座城市比喀什更顯得緊張不安。雖然如此，普遍來說，還是比我二〇一八年的前次訪問時，放鬆多了。

我們行經城市外緣的一家博物館，剛好館內舉辦一場展覽，內容與一九六二年中印邊界的小規模軍事衝突相關。在我們前進西藏之前，即將要再度趨近這塊熱點區域，於是，我們來去匆匆地參

Moon Chin on left of C-53 Kunlun / 陳文寬在 C-53( 左 ) 喀喇崑崙山
Sea container hotel / 海運貨櫃飯店
Karakoram near K2 / 喀喇崑崙山接近 K2

觀了博物館，博物館的院子裡，還擺放一台年代久遠、「功成身退」的坦克車。

身為長期熱衷且關切中國當代軍事歷史的觀察者來說，我犯上了「職業病」而忍不住在博物館展示中挑出小錯誤。比方說，描述戰爭前線的圖片上一台「北京 212 吉普車」，其實那款吉普車遲至一九六五年才生產，但博物館卻誤置這台吉普車曾在一九六二年的戰爭中派上用場。我對這款車型的生產史瞭若指掌，因為我曾於一九七九年親自訪視位於北京的吉普車工廠。同理推算，展示圖片上介紹的解放牌卡車，極有可能也是出自後期的照片。雖然如此，這些小瑕疵並未削弱展示的主題與目標。

下一站，是行經 219 國道，從葉城到阿克賽欽 (Aksai Chin) 將近六百公里的漫漫長途，大約需要十六小時車程。我們在路上停靠塔吉克人的小社區柯克亞 (Kekeya)，吃頓午餐，也把車子加滿油，再上路。看似尋常的一段路，但其實這是一段歷史上的商隊路線，由此通往與來回中國的帕米爾高原。

我們的後勤部經理李娜，趁此難得機會，在當地購買與蒐集了幾項手工刺繡的婦女帽，作為我們的展覽文物，而措姆則忙著與當地女性朋友進行現場訪談，一刻不得閒。當六十歲的塔吉克婦女泰吉古莉發現我們對她的手工編織帽愛不釋手時，她立即衝回家去，又拿了兩頂較新的帽子；但泰吉古莉有所不知，其實我們比較鍾意的是那兩頂舊款帽，尤其是女主人頭上戴的那頂。

姿瓦古麗，今年二十歲，來自柯克亞社區五座村莊中的第五村，在我們半途停靠吃午餐的餐廳裡當兼職服務生。她的五口之家，在當地算是一般普通家庭的縮影，家人畜養了三百隻綿羊與二十五頭犛牛。五座村莊裡總共有九十九戶家庭，總人口是三百一十九，平均每戶三人左右。整個社區清一色是塔吉克人，沒有任何外來族群。

離開柯克亞社區，我們陸續穿越四大雪域山口，雖是坐在車裡，但眼前冰雪漫天蓋地，一路迎風、冒雪、再頂著冰雹，從新疆到西藏——這段起伏的綿延長路，從平地沙漠到地表上最高的高原，可說是跨越兩極化地域與文化過渡的最佳詮釋。我們從沙漠植物白楊樹與紅柳樹、以及偶爾瞥見的綿羊與駱駝等典型風沙荒漠的景物，一路到嚴寒高地，所有地形與風貌，也跟著轉換成高寒灌木叢與成群的犛牛之鄉。我們也從天差地遠的地貌，跨越到徹底不同的文化，從塔吉克人與維吾爾族的伊斯蘭國度，跨越到以佛教為主的西藏。

沿途中，為了「步步高升」以增加海拔高度，我們經過其中一段最長的迴旋路段。在我們右邊，或說是朝南的喀喇崑崙山，最突出的，是 8611 公尺的最高主峰——喬戈里峰 (K2)。位居世界第二高峰的喬戈里峰，同時也是地表上登山罹難死亡率第二高的山峰。喬戈里峰的陡峭與艱難險阻，對登山者是無人不知的「高」難度。根據報導，在試圖登頂的人中，大約有百分之二十五的登山者，壯志未酬身先死。不管哪一年，如果申請攀登珠穆朗瑪峰的登山者有五百人的話，那麼，申請攀登喬戈里峰的登山客，一年裡可能寥寥無幾，乏人問津。

我想起今年初高齡一〇九歲的好朋友陳文寬隊長曾完成的其中一項壯舉。在二戰期間的一九四二年六月，陳文寬開著 C-53( 航空史最具代表性的 DC-3 運輸機改良版 )，從新疆的葉爾羌成功飛越喬戈里峰附近的喀喇崑崙山，降落於當時的印度領土白沙瓦 (Peshawar)，白沙瓦現在已屬於巴基斯坦。這條西部駝峰航線，是規劃好的替代飛行航徑，以防備日本軍在佔領整個緬甸區域後，關閉喜馬拉雅山脈東部的駝峰航線。美國空軍曾多次嘗試以更先進的 C-87 飛機試圖從印度穿越喀喇崑崙山，飛入中國新疆，但都無功而返，一直到陳文寬授命承擔起這份重責大任後，終於成功完成這項近乎無望的使命。

以我個人的經歷來說，一如以往嘗試了好幾次，我再度鎩羽而歸，無法如願進入喀喇崑崙山口——一條連接到克什米爾的歷史性商隊路線。這個掌握通道的山口，曾是中國、巴基斯坦與印度之間的貿易前哨站，現在已成為邊界區域的軍事熱點。既然此路不通，我便隨遇而安，在通往邊境的叉路口，找個地方過一夜，撫慰一下自己的悵然若失。這家剛開業的旅社，由海運物流的集裝箱堆積而成，這讓我們這群遠離海洋十萬八千里的旅人看來，顯得有些突兀而不尋常。

我們另外也在邊界處發現一間軍事急救診所。我的牙痛似乎與節節高升的海拔高度「相得益彰」，越高越疼，於是，我走進這家解放軍的診所，從身穿迷彩服、彬彬有禮的醫護人員手中取得免費的止痛藥，舒緩一下我的疼痛症狀。

紅土山口分別標示了兩個海拔高度，5347 公尺與 5380 公尺，由此進入阿克賽欽。見我們團隊成員各個冷得層層包裹在羽絨外套下，我趁此大好機會，拍下照片寄給遙遠的南方友人，此時當下，我

Tibetan Antelope taken by drone / 無人機拍攝的藏羚羊

Wild Ass at foothill / 山麓上的野驢

的南方朋友在急速暖化的炎炎烈日下，過他們的盛暑夏日。我們所在的這塊土地，極其遼闊，佔地約 38000 平方公里，相當於一個不丹國的面積，比台灣稍微大一些，大部分高度平均都在 5000 公尺以上。以行政區域來說，這地方隸屬新疆的和田，但在地理位置上，它是青藏高原的延伸。雖然一切都牢牢掌控在中國手中，但長久以來卻經常引發中國與印度兩國之間的主權爭議。

一九五〇年末，中方修建了一條從新疆直達西藏的道路，顯然這是高具戰略意義的行動；一九六二年，中國的這項軍事部署隨即引發兩國之間長達一個月的戰事。其實，這地方原來是荒蕪之地，名副其實的「無邊無界」，疆界模糊，自然動輒升級為政治主權之爭，而且因為杳無人煙，更是雙方軍事對抗，戰炮轟鳴的最佳場地。戰爭結束後，中國就此永久掌控了這片區域。

青藏高原的野生動物，也陸續顯露蹤跡，先是少數動物零星出沒；然後，越來越多，最後甚至成群結隊，隨處可見。其中有野驢、藏羚羊，幸運的話，偶爾還可看見藏原羚。有一次，我們在途中與一大群母羚羊不期而遇，驚鴻一瞥，其數約上百隻；這群藏羚羊很可能已開始長途遷徙一段時間，準備找個隱蔽好地，在六月中旬與七月初之間產下牠們的羚羊寶寶。

現在，每每在這些荒蕪高地看見一群群動物遊蕩路邊，面對路人也無所畏懼、視而不見，我心中的欣慰，難以言喻。人畜之間的和諧共處，正好說明了政府的保護工作都已初見效果，其中包括多年來對動物保護的意識與教育的提升，以及嚴格處分盜獵的法規與成效，都令人欣慰。更令我們團隊驚訝的是，即時我們啟動無人機準備高空拍攝，即時無人機已在這群藏羚羊頭上嗡嗡趨近，這群老神在在的羚羊，竟聞聲而不動，一副沒啥大驚小怪的模樣，繼續埋頭吃草去。

從喀什出發，行經三天三夜的車程，眼前一座橫跨公路的高聳紀念碑的大門，昭告所有旅人——已平安抵達西藏。這樣一段三天的旅程，對一百年前的商隊來說，至少要披星戴月耗時一個月，才能抵達目的地。我們雖已抵達西藏，但要從這裡前往拉薩，還需要再三、四天車程；若再換算成商隊的顛簸之旅，那又是另一個月的餐風露宿了。

今天，我們的旅行模式越來越講究速度與效率，但我憂心的是，我們旅遊體驗之深與廣，已變得越來越膚淺散漫。藉由閱讀一些過去的書籍，幫助我把空白的鴻溝填補起來，讓我有所餘裕，去欣賞一段緩慢流動的時間，與距離遙遙相隔的世代。

Aksai Chin / 阿克賽欽

從喀什到拉薩（下集）

# KASHGAR TO LHASA (Part 2)

Lhasa, Tibet – June 2, 2022

Lhasa, Tibet – June 2, 2022

*KASHGAR TO LHASA (Part 2)*

*The descent from over 5000 meters to 4500 is gradual but welcomed. Adding whatever amount of oxygen to such rarefied air is much appreciated. My breathing pattern begins to feel lighter, and the drowsiness caused by lack of oxygen is relieved. I no longer choke from speaking half a sentence, gasping for air before finishing. 4500 meters is still a forbidding height for many people. My team, however, have been well acclimatized, not to mention that three of them are Tibetans.*

*Pangong Tso is the first sizable lake we come upon after leaving Xinjiang. This elongated lake, some 160 kilometers in length, cuts through China's border into India. As both India and China describe the lake in overview, the freshwater eastern two-thirds is on the China side, whereas the salty western one-third lies inside India's territory. Online, there are claims this is the largest saltwater lake in India. True only if one ignores the large amount of freshwater on the other side of the border.*

*Such aberration is common when we each look at the world from within our own frame of reference. This notion can also be applied to many religions concerning which mountain is the most sacred, as each beholder has his or her own opinion and conviction. National border lines are another analogy, perhaps better left for each country's leaders, manifest through their militaries and politicians, to* define. Pangong Tso has come to fit that last analogy squarely over the last few years. The agreed description of one-third in India and two-thirds in China becomes contending measurements of kilometers, meters, and fractions thereof when on the ground.

Surpassing the elevation of the lake's altitude, I reached a different attitude when I first viewed Pangong Tso.... from space. In the early to mid-1980s, I had the great good fortune to work with remote sensing scientists at NASA's Jet Propulsion Laboratory in Pasadena California, just below my mountain cabin home. It fascinated me when I beheld an image of western Tibet taken with hand-held camera by an astronaut. That image, now within our archive of photos, shows Pangong Tso among the majestic Himalayas cutting a swath over the curvature of our earth. That special scene from space is still imprinted on my mind to this day.

It wasn't until 1993 that I finally set foot on the lakefront of Pangong Tso and then dipped my feet, and then my body, into its chilling water. The lake was desolate and no tourists or military personnel were around, unlike today. Washing our Land Rovers by driving into the lake would no doubt be considered criminal in this day and age. In a nearby village, I was even able to interview an older Tibetan who had served as a guide to the PLA during the 1962 frontier war.

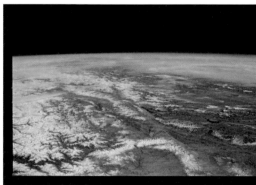

Close up of Pangong lake from space /
從太空近看班公錯胡
Shuttle hand-held photo with long lake on right /
太空梭上手持式相機拍攝長湖於右側

Tibetan guide of 1962 battle /
西藏響導導覽 1962 戰爭

I went a second time in 1999, and we chartered a motorized boat and scouted the bird island. It was at a time during the breeding season of migratory birds. Bird nests, predominantly of the Brown-headed Gull, were so abundant that we had to pace the ground carefully lest our feet step on the young chicks or brooding parents.

Today, no one is allowed to visit the bird island except perhaps scientists. Motorized boats charging a steep fee only take visitors to look from a respectable distance away from the island. During my other visits, in 2006 and most recently in 2018, there were still several families operating restaurants serving up large lake fish they caught with nets. All that has disappeared today. In its place are new buildings as rest areas for the many tourists in self-driven cars now vacationing here, as throughout China.

We chose a hidden cove by the lake, and I spent a quiet day adding sun to my already tanned body to gain more bragging rights when I return home. Nearby, there were plenty of waterfowl, including the Bar-headed Geese with their new chicks following. The Brown-headed Gull were most abundant as before, now becoming beggars, as they have gotten used to so many passers-by tourists feeding them.

My time in Tibet was necessarily short, after expanding and stretching *my time in Xinjiang.  From Pangong Tso we drove into Ngari and had an evening of rest.  I was surprised to see the growing prefecture town now had an entire Uighur street where there were many restaurants serving Islamic cuisine.  Naturally, we took the opportunity to try them out.*

*Next stop – Kailash, the most sacred mountain for Tibetans and Hindus alike, and the adjacent sacred Lake Manasarovar.  The area is considered by many as the navel of the world.  My first circumambulation of Kailash was exactly twenty years ago, during the year of the Horse.  On such an auspicious year, one circuit around the 53-kilometer route counts as 13, so I am good, not having to repeat the feat for a while.  After all, the starting point is 4600 meters in elevation, with two passes rising far above 5000 meters.  Drolma Pass is at 5600 meters, rather formidable for someone over 70 like myself.*

*However, my team, especially the younger ones, are all eager to make the circuit.  Three of them are Tibetans, Drolma had done it together with Li Na in 2018 when I last came through.  But for Tsomo and Lobsang, they have yet to make their first pilgrimage.  Finally, five out of my team of eight left in the wee hours of the night to begin*

Camping at lakefront 1993 / 湖前紮營於 1993 年

Washing cars on lake 1993 / 湖裡洗車於 1933 年

*their circumambulation, hoping to finish around midnight.*

*I satisfied myself in adding yet another layer of tan, sitting by the lake, and hiding in the camper van whenever I get drowsy. But the distant view of Mount Kailash to my north and Mount Gurla Mandhata, a 7,694 meter mountain to my south across the lake, kept me outdoors most of the time. The latter, considered the highest peak in the western Himalayas, defines the border between China and Nepal. Nearby my camp, Tibetan pilgrims came to add a few more stones onto the mani pile of prayer stones along the lakefront. Many of the stones were carved with the inscription Om Mani Padme Hum, meaning "Hail to the jewel in the lotus."*

*Around the lake were several temples and shrines, seven in all I believe. Formerly attached to the Drukpa Kargyu lineage within Tibetan Buddhism, they had been forcefully taken over since 2014 by the Karma Kargyu, a larger and more dominating branch of the Kargyu sect. The contention remains to this day.*

*The world is more focused, or interested, in the contest and conflict, real or imagined, of the government of China with each and every religion. Few would bother to delve into the internal strife within each religion. After all, such matters are not fodder for discrediting China. As I know from my journalistic training, modus operandi for our profession is that problems reported make good news. Happy endings rarely, if ever, gather attention and usually go unreported.*

Gurla Mandhata with sacred lake Manasorora in front / 納木那尼峰和緊鄰的瑪旁雍錯湖

The five pilgrims in my team returned to our camp midmorning the following day. To say that they were exhausted is an understatement. But spiritually they are certainly enlivened and looked jubilant. I shared their joy and rejuvenated them by offering some cold beer and snacks. The beer just may have made them feel even higher, in spirit and in elevation.

What would have taken a week in the past, from Kailash to Lhasa, has now been reduced to two days on all-paved road. More and more, we ran into self-driving tourists in private cars, predominantly SUVs or 4x4, many converted to the heels. One exceptional sight was a Tesla, pulled by a car in front with a rope. Obviously, the battery had run out, but the next charging station was not far away; just over the horizon.

Our last stop before Lhasa was the ancient Sakya Monastery, head monastery of one of the four main sects of Tibetan Buddhism. It was first founded in the year 1073. Today, the ensemble of buildings is a sight to behold, spanning both sides of the Zhongqu River and spreading high up into the hill. I had only visited it once, over twenty years ago. That is unusual and not good, as ancient monasteries seem to have a magnetic effect on me.

A couple of phone calls to Rinpoche friends and the problem was quickly settled. The head monk would meet me and host my visit. Not only that, a young and very knowledgeable monk was put at our disposal as our guide. With many Tibetan pilgrims at the monastery, we received very special treatment and I was given the "ok" to photograph anything at will, including some of the beautiful murals.

We were led through a hidden enclave behind the main Assembly Hall. The huge library of sutras inside was phenomenal, boasting the largest such collection in the entire Tibetan region. The knowledge within covers the most extensive disciplines of study, both religious and secular, on the high plateau. Texts stacked from floor to ceiling, tens of thousands in all, covered an entire back side of a long room. There were some rare volumes inscribed on palm leaves, and one particular volume, put behind a glass case, was purportedly the largest hand-written Tibetan sutra in the world. It measured 1.34 meters long, 1.09 meters wide, and 67 centimeters thick, and the writings were inscribed in gold.

Not only did the head monk Kengpo Lodro Gyatso receive us warmly with silk khata, my first greeting with him, by touching heads, was something offered only to someone with high honor or between high monks and among Rinpoche. Given my cursory knowledge of Tibetan Buddhism, this moment was both gracious and elevating. We parted ways after receiving many gifts, including a small statue for me, and sacred incense made at the monastery for each and every member of our team.

Alas, Lhasa was reached, after over two months on the road. We stayed, as always, at my friend's very fine Shambala Boutique Hotel right around the corner from the Barkhor, a circular street in the heart of old town Lhasa. Tibetan pilgrims come from far and wide to tread the Barkhor's stones, circumambulating around the most sacred Jokhang Temple.

While taking a hiatus in Lhasa, we were introduced to the young general secretary Chime Tserang who was recently assigned to administer the old town and in particular the Barkhor region. He led me through some newly installed exhibits about old town, especially regarding its past. I suddenly thought of the best gift to offer to this

Buildings of Sakya Monastery / 薩迦寺建築物
Sakya Monastery library of sutras /
薩迦寺的佛經圖書館

ancient religious center, mecca for the entire Tibetan Plateau.

During my many trips to Lhasa, starting from 1982 while working for the National Geographic, I had taken hundreds, if not thousands, of photographs of old Lhasa. Back in those days, before digital photography and smart-phone cameras, hardly anyone was able to afford as many rolls of film as I had. Our archive of some very fine photographs of Lhasa from the early 1980s and through the two decades of my many visits would be most valuable for enriching the documentation of this now flourishing capital of Tibet.

On the day I left Lhasa, Chime came over to our hotel and I personally handed over to him a tiny USB drive. This was our first batch of Lhasa photographs, some 650 images in all, from my first visit in 1982, downloaded from my computer. While these were not high-resolution images, they were nonetheless of great value to Lhasa city itself. I promised, when time permitted, that I would send more pictures from my subsequent trips.

Such a modest act of giving is perhaps the best way to end my long journey from Kashgar to Lhasa.

Potala in Lhasa / 拉薩的布達拉宮

Bird Island 1999 / 鳥島於 1999 年

直到一九九三年，我才終於「腳踏實地」，站在班公錯湖畔，然後，雙腳踩進湖水裡，慢慢再讓全身浸入冰冷的湖水中。當時的湖泊荒涼寂靜，周遭沒有任何遊客或軍人，和今天景況大不同。今天，如果把我們的「路華」越野車開進湖裡洗一洗，肯定會被視為現行犯。我在附近的村莊採訪了一位老藏族，他曾於一九六二年在中印邊界戰事中擔任過解放軍的嚮導。

一九九九年，我再度重訪。那一次，我們租了一艘摩托船環湖探察鳥島。當時正值候鳥的繁殖期。以棕頭鷗為主的鳥巢，多得俯拾皆是，我們不得不如履薄冰，小心慢走，以免誤踩到待在鳥巢裡的雛鳥或正在餵食的母鳥。

今天，除了做研究的科學家之外，鳥島已嚴禁外人入內；遊客只准搭乘收費高昂的摩托船，在離島甚遠之處「遠觀」。我後來陸續在二〇〇六與最近的二〇一八年舊地重遊，當時附近還有幾間家庭經營的餐廳，把他們從大湖裡網捕的魚做成湖鮮料理，吸引遊客。時過境遷，這些過去都已不復見，取而代之的是一棟棟新建築，作為來此度假的自駕遊客量身打造的休息區，一如中國其他各地一樣。

我們選了湖邊一個隱蔽的水彎，我清閑無事，過了安靜自在的一天，不管身體早已曬了一圈黑，我恣意躺在陽光下，繼續曬；這

Brown-headed Gulls in flight / 空中的棕頭鷗
Gulls with chicks on Bird Island / 鳥島上的棕頭鷗與幼鳥

在拉薩短暫的放空期間，經介紹而結識了年輕的書記代表曲美次仁 (Chime Tserang)，他最近被派駐管理老城區，尤以八廓區為主。他帶我參觀一些最近才開設的展覽，展覽主題與老城區的歷史有關。這趟展覽使我靈光乍現，我忽然想到自己可以為這個古老的宗教中心——整個青藏高原的「聖地」——貢獻一份意義不凡的絕佳禮物。

從一九八二年投身美國《國家地理雜誌》的工作開始，我陸續前往拉薩許多次，也拍攝了上百張、甚至數千張過去的拉薩照片。回望那段數位相機與智能手機還沒出現的日子，很少有人能像我那樣，買得起那麼多膠卷底片。我的圖像檔案裡，至今仍保有一些非常完整的拉薩舊照，這些都是我從一九八〇年代初期至後續二十幾年來，多次訪問拉薩時拍攝的；這對於越來越欣欣向榮的西藏首都來說，無疑是饒富價值的紀錄與文獻。

離開拉薩那天，曲美先生到我們的飯店來，我親手把一個小小隨身碟交給他，檔案內容是第一批拉薩的照片，那是我一九八二年初訪拉薩時，拍下的六百五十張照片，從我的電腦圖庫下載到隨身碟。雖然老照片不具高解析度，但這些影像紀錄對拉薩的歷史貢獻，有很大的價值。我答應他，只要時間允許，我一定會在後續的旅途中把更多圖檔寄給他。

從喀什到拉薩這段漫漫長路，最終以一分微不足道的分享畫下旅途句點，或許也是一種好方法。

Kengpo Lodro with HM / 勘布羅卓和 HM

白
瑪
崗

# PEMAKO

Medog, Tibet – June 7, 2022

Mother and child Bodeng / 波東村的母親和小孩

Weaver of Bodong / 波東村的紡織者

*holidays, Dawa had to help in chores at home, harvesting corn and planting rice, with two seasons each year, thus keeping him busy both during summer and winter vacations. Such work left Dawa little time for study. His parents died when he was young and he grew up with his elder sister and brother-in-law.*

*Upon graduation from a vocational school in Kunming, Dawa changed jobs several times locally in Medog. In October last year, he met Zhou Yushu who was in charge of building and organizing the moving of villagers to the new village. Dawa learned cooking from Zhou and became the chef of the lodge, earning around 3000 Yuan a month. With housing and meals supplied, he finally managed to save up some money. For the three days we stayed at the lodge, Dawa cooked some of our most palatable meals in this faraway distant enclave.*

*Many of the villages we visited are within Beibeng Township, an administrative zone which encompasses several smaller villages. They include Badeng, Achong, Xiyan and De'ergong. In places, we can compare new villages to nearby abandoned old ones. But of particular interest to me is Bodong, an old village still in use, though the new one is almost complete and ready for moving in. Old Bodong offers a glimpse into the conditions of the Monpa's former architecture, lifestyle and standard of living. Most families are engaged in weaving handicrafts. Describing old Bodong, besides saying it is squalid, I can borrow a cliché often used by new-age foodies - very "organic." "Sustainable" is perhaps inappropriate, since it will soon be moved.*

*Away from all these Monpa villages and to the north at a junction from the gushing Brahmaputra* is Damu Xin Cun, a newly built Lhoba Village. As Medog's only gas station has run out of diesel fuel, our Land Rover could barely get back to Bomi, with the gauge showing near empty. So we could only dispatch our other car into Damu. Two of us in team and I opted to stay behind and wait.

Within two hours, our remaining team of six returned with many surprises; a motherlode of Lhoba artifacts, including some tied to the roof. This had to be our most successful collecting trip, all within a matter of hours. Li Na, our chief artifact collector, had managed to nail down the retired village chief Tashi. He had a private exhibit of Lhoba artifacts and crafts, including many hunting trophy of animals. Showing her charm and finesse in negotiation, Li Na was able to purchase many of his personal items.

Our exit and return drive to Bomi was late in the afternoon. I absorbed myself in enjoying the many waterfalls, sheer mountains and snowfields. As we crossed again the long tunnel to the north slope of the Himalayas range, it felt like we had left the beyul paradise behind. The yellow light on the fuel gauge of my Land Rover had long been lit up when I saw the first gas station sign. I pushed the fuel/distance button and saw that what remained in the tank was good for only four kilometers. While my car was thirsting for a refuel, I have quenched myself in fulfilling a long dream of visiting this hidden enclave of the Tibetan plateau.

# 白瑪崗

## 西藏的隱秘山谷

過去三天裡，我每天清晨與傍晚所聽到的，或許就是我稱之為「森林之歌」的樂音吧。薄暮黃昏時，夾雜著蟋蟀唧唧的蟲鳴，仿若此起彼落的合唱曲，不絕於耳。如果我用兩手摀著耳朵，反而感覺聲量更大了，猶如露天劇場傳來般，悅耳動聽。晨間時分，蟲鳴合唱轉為低沈音色，鳥聲啁啾，跟著新的旋律高低起伏，而洋洋盈耳。有些從低音吟唱起，節節升高，抵達最高音時，瞬間戛然而止。而叢林中的氤氳之氣與薄霧，則是這天然劇院的舞台佈景。

餘音繞梁的天然音樂會，是我深入墨脫縣 (Medog) 中心──連結中國公路的最後一個縣鎮──才能享有的饗宴。墨脫縣是中國在喜馬拉雅山以南唯一的縣鎮，四年前的二〇一八年接上公路時，頓成大家津津樂道的建設大事。從喜馬拉雅山脈北麓東段最靠近的波密縣出發，得經過一條長約 110 多公里的蜿蜒公路，穿越中間一道三公里左右的隧道，隧道貫穿一座山脈，繞過山頂長年積雪的山峰、冰川，和一座隨時會發生雪崩的雪場。

雖然如此，有些地方的雪場就在公路旁，或深入附近的常綠森林中。這些地方隨處可見五彩經幡，隨風飄揚；可想而知，當地人試圖以宗教的超自然力量，來安撫與平息大自然中殘酷的破壞力。在其他不同地方，車子開在這條通道上，彷彿行駛於奔流不息的溪水中，期間偶爾還會跨越鋪天蓋地的狀況——雪崩或落石坍方可能像傾瀉而下的瀑布般，令人望而生畏。

這條路只有單向道，因此，偶數日開放入境，單數日則開放出境。這也是中國唯一一個要收費才能駛入的城鎮，除了當地居民或公務在身人員，其他外人則一律收費 210 人民幣。還有另一個免收費的條件——七十歲以上長者。因此，我成為我們一行九人團隊中唯一免費入境者。

從將近 4000 公尺高的波密高山，我們穿過隧道後，一路蜿蜒而下，經過雨林生態系統，我們抵達 1000 公尺海拔以下的墨脫縣。這是我遊走西藏四十多年來，親眼瞥見的第一片水稻田。緊隨稻田後，陸續出現其他熱帶雨林植被，譬如香蕉園、木瓜園甚至茶園。我們經過一個村莊，路邊不少攤販都在擺賣當地的農作物與編織等手工藝品。

按著過去的歷史，這區域被居住在喜馬拉雅山麓的藏族與其他人稱為白瑪崗 (Pemako)。這裡所謂的「其他人」指的是中國的門巴族 (Monpa) 與珞巴族 (Lhoba)，門巴族總人口大約是一萬人，而珞巴族更少，只有四千人左右。當然，這個人口數據不包括印度領土的同種族人。

Icefields and glaciers / 冰原和冰河

自有歷史紀錄以來，門巴族就一直住在這地方，他們在文化與宗教方面，其實與藏族沒什麼差別，只是生活方式比較不同；門巴族的安身之地是小塊小塊平地的深山老林，而非高原上。浪漫而滿懷詩意的六世達賴喇嘛就是門巴族，出生自西部達旺 (Tawang) 鎮，就在不丹國的東邊。也有人相信，今天的許多門巴族其實來自不丹東部的流亡人士與移民。「中國探險學會」曾訪問過不丹南部一個大約三百人、也叫「門巴」的小部落，在當地進行人種學方面的質性研究。不過，迄今為止，還無法釐清這個群體，到底與生活在印度控管區達旺鎮和西藏墨脫縣的門巴族之間，有何關聯。

我有幸在一九八七年訪問過珞巴族，他們其實很接近察隅縣的僜人──僜人也是喜馬拉雅山南麓的米什米 (Mishimi) 支派之一。珞巴族主要靠狩獵為生，擅用弓箭，而且天生篤信大自然神祇、對自然神力崇敬有加。我曾以動態錄影，拍攝他們的狩獵行動，也曾親眼觀察他們宰殺雞隻後取其骨，再把穀物放在雞骨上進行算命雞卜儀式。不過，這一切都已是三十五年前的往事了。

Flooded road / 被淹沒的道路　　　　　Fortune-telling with chicken 1987 / 用雞 卜卦於 1987 年

所謂「隱密山谷」(beyul)，其原意是「應許的隱密地」，有些類似「香格里拉、伊甸園與桃花源」等理想境地集於一身的象徵意涵。據說，西藏高原上有三大主要的「隱密山谷」，包括我們最近去過、位於西藏西部的岡仁波齊峰，另外兩處，分別是神秘詩聖密勒日巴 (Milarepa) 曾在尼泊爾暫居的拉布吉山谷 (Lapchi)，以及靠近墨脫縣的桀日 (Tsari)，桀日的別名就是白瑪崗。

作為喜馬拉雅山以南的邊境區域，墨 鎮無疑是中國的戰略重鎮，是印度與中國之間一觸即發的引爆熱點，因而更加劇此地的軍事化色彩。英國記者馬克斯維爾 (Neville Maxwell) 曾在他的著作《印度對華戰爭》(India's War with China) 中敘述兩國之間於一九六二年引發的邊界戰事。雖然中印關係張力不斷，但對研究動物與植物領域的專家來說，這個兵家必爭之地，是生物學家的多元物種瑰寶，因為鮮有外人踏足而益顯彌足珍貴；尤其是昆蟲學家，這地方簡直是他們的研究天堂。

不過，對深入其中的我們來說，眼前的實況與風花雪月的詩意樂園，豈止天壤之別。雨季已經開始，叢林內大量水蛭蠢蠢欲動，蓄勢待發。我們一行人穿越一座臨時搭建的吊橋，緊跟著一名森林嚮導，

Bridge enroute to Lobang monastery / 通往 Lobang 寺的橋

Team with tapped gaiters / 團隊用膠布捆腳

Dawa at lodge kitchen / 達瓦在民宿的廚房

前往參觀邊境區一座廢棄的 *Lobang* 寺。儘管大夥兒都在腿上纏裹膠布，層層包覆，但小 *Drolma* 在兩小時的徒步遊走回來時，腿上已被七條水蛭牢牢吸附，滿載而歸。我提醒她，傳統中國醫學使用水蛭來為病患放血，在西方醫學，水蛭則被當成麻醉劑的研究。於是，我們決定把這幾隻戰利品放置瓶罐裡，以茲紀念，也作為我們的研究標本。

我們住在新蓋的巴登村，這個偏遠小村離邊界不遠，跨過軍事哨站後方、橫渡雅魯藏布江上的一座橋之外。這條西藏雄偉而水流湍急的母親河，匯入印度與孟加拉平原而成布拉馬普特拉河之前，因急轉彎而海拔高度陡然下降。因為坡度陡降而匯聚成大瀑布，一直是個傳說，流傳了一個多世紀仍為人津津樂道，但經直升機的實地搜尋與偵察，外加衛星圖像的佐證，終於說服大家，所謂大瀑布，其實沒有那麼大。

巴登村是去年八月才蓋好的村莊，現在已有三十八戶人家，總共是一百八十四名門巴族人定居於此。村內有三棟房子，作為門巴族旅館，由村莊委員會所擁有與經營管理。其他邊境附近的，除了波東村以外，都是以被被政府新建工程取代的老村落。事實上，波東村也很快要遷村了。未來政府分配的房子，屋型空間各有大小，取決於家庭成員的多寡。家家戶戶都有個小院子，一廳一廚一衛，臥房則分為一間或好幾間的格局。我們在波東村參訪時，還可一瞥過去傳統的舊木房，相較之下，新式的房子衛生條件與設備已改善很多。今天，許多村民不只從事農業生產，同時也種茶，額外收入大大提升了他們的生活品質。

我們的「田野民族研究學者」Tsomo 女士採訪了兩名門巴族的旅館工作人員。她的發現或許能說明過去的一些情境。受訪者之一的達瓦仁欽 (Dawa Rinchen)，今年三十四歲，從老波東村搬到這裡來。憶起自己的童年時，就讀小學的他，每天都得帶著穀類、油、鹽與胡椒到學校。每一個星期，老師會給每一位學生分配三十公斤大米，孩子們便需要自己煮午餐。路途遙遠，每日每夜，達瓦都得徒步往返學校。

Monpa new village / 門巴族的新村

等到他升學到初中的寄宿學校時，他的家庭已漸入佳境，不再需要自備食物了。但到週末時，寄宿學校只提供早晚兩餐，午餐自理。達瓦通常會和同學爬上山，到野外採集，覓食解饑。達瓦偶爾也會從家裡帶一兩公斤的大米到學校，有時甚至還會借老師的爐灶自己做飯。

每學期結束前，所有學生都必須同心協力到處收集木柴供應學校的食堂，確保新的下學期學校有烹煮的「柴料」可用。一般來說，每一個學生必須在學期放假前完成每人數十公斤的「找柴」指標。放假期間，達瓦則要留在家裡操持家務，還要收割玉米與種水稻；

一年兩季的農忙，讓達瓦的寒暑假都不得閒。馬不停蹄的農忙幾乎讓他沒時間好好學習。達瓦還小時，父母便已相繼離世，他在姊姊與姊夫的照顧下長大。

從昆明的一所職業學校畢業後，達瓦在墨脫縣城換了幾份工作。去年十月，他認識了負責建設與組織村民遷村工作的周玉恕。達瓦向周玉恕學烹飪，成了他們工作室的廚師，每月收入約 3000 人民幣。因為有免費的住宿與膳食供應，達瓦終於可以設法存錢了。我們一行人住在偏遠飛地山莊的那三天，達瓦為我們這群遠道而來的外來客親自下廚，端上當地的美味佳餚。

我們訪問的許多村莊都在背崩鄉內，背崩鄉是個行政區域，其中包括幾個小村莊——巴登村、阿蒼村、西讓村與德爾貢村。有些地方還可以看到棄置的舊村廢墟，新舊並存，一眼便可看出其中差異。但我特別感興趣的是波東村，雖然全新的已幾乎竣工、準備開放入住，但其中一間還在使用中的舊村莊特別引起我的注意。舊波東村讓人得以從一磚一瓦一橫樑中瞥見門巴族的老建築、過去的生活方式與生活水平等實況。大部分家庭以從事編織手工藝為主。若要用什麼詞彙來形容舊波東，除了「凌亂」這詞，我還可以借用新世代美食家愛用的老套形容詞——非常「有機」。我想「永續」這詞或許不太合宜，因為村里之間很快就要進行搬移遷村了。

離開門巴族村莊，我們沿著洶湧澎湃的布拉馬普特拉河往北前進，抵達一個路口處，那是剛建好的珞巴族村落——達木新村。由於墨脫縣唯一的加油站柴油供應已用罄，我們的「荒原路華」越野車，也只能勉為其難的回到波密，油表顯示已接近空箱。我們無計可施，只能派另一輛車到達木新村，由我和團隊中的另外倆人，一起留在當地等待。

不到兩小時，其他六位團員帶著許多令人詫異的驚喜回來——大量珞巴族文物，還包括一些綁在車頂的東西。這可算是此趟旅程中最「豐收」的一次，而且就在短短幾小時內發生。我們的文物收藏主任李娜，費盡心機終於找到當地的一位退休村長，塔希。塔希有個不對外開放的私人珞巴族文物與手工藝品展示室，包括他們狩獵的戰利品。李娜把她的專業魅力與談判技巧派上用場，成功說服這位當地耆老，如願購入許多原屬非賣品的文物。

離開當地，開車返回波密時，已接近午後了。我全神貫注地欣賞沿途的許多瀑布、陡峭霸氣的山峰與雪地冰原。當我們再度穿越通往喜馬拉雅山北坡的狹長隧道時，我覺得自己似乎已漸漸遠離「隱秘山谷」的天堂樂園。抬眼一見加油站標誌時，我的路華越野車的油表，也已亮起黃燈。我按下「燃料／距離」按鈕，檢視一下油箱，發現剩下的油只夠我們再開四公里。顯然我的車子已飢渴難耐，但我已滿足了一償宿願的渴望——如願實地探查青藏高原上這塊隱密飛地的夢想。

Bodong village / 波東村

Tashi with family / 扎西和家人

Animal trophies / 動物戰利品

南西嶺皇宮與不丹皇太后陛下

# NAMSEYLING PALACE & HER MAJESTY THE ROYAL GRANDMOTHER OF BHUTAN

Namseyling, Bhutan – September 4, 2022

## NAMSEYLING PALACE & HER MAJESTY THE ROYAL GRANDMOTHER OF BHUTAN

*My caution and hesitation now seem premature and unfounded. When first asked to use Namseyling Palace, once home to the late mother of the 92-years-old Royal Grandmother of Bhutan, I had reservations and doubts, feeling underserving. "I hope you will like Namseyling," Her Majesty told me several times. At first, I wondered if I had heard Her Majesty's message correctly. After all, she always speaks with such a soft and tender voice. It is like whispering into one's ears.*

*But this offer had been repeated multiple times whenever I had the occasion to meet Her Majesty at her palace. In between visits, Ashi Kesang, Her Majesty's granddaughter, showed me Namseyling Palace twice when I visited Bhutan. It was like a small museum with many historic photos and artifacts, being home of Her Majesty's late mother Rani Chuni Wangmo Dorji. Yet no one had lived there since the 1970s, or perhaps only briefly in the 1980s. Otherwise, only deities reside at Namseyling Palace. Ashi Kesang mentioned time and again that the invitation was genuine and real, not a casual impromptu offer.*

*I began to think seriously about how to take up such a royal invitation in a deserving way. My mother has always taught me, "if you cannot give back, do not take". This had become a quiet motto I tried to live by. I interpreted that "giving back" as meaning not necessarily to the exact person*

Namseyling Palace / 南西嶺皇宮

I took from, but extended more generally to giving back to "others". With that context, I had found an equitable balance between taking and giving, using CERS as a conduit.

I left Hong Kong August 29. After an overnight layover in Bangkok, I boarded a 7 am DrukAir flight onward to Bhutan. The figure 8 visual circuit pattern snaking through green mountains on the descent approach to Paro Airport was no longer a hair-raising surprise, but a much looked-forward-to joyride, as I admired the smooth and precision maneuver by captain of the airplane. Going through immigration was smooth and fast, though preceded by the much longer Covid swab test and form filling.

The capital Thimphu was about an hour's drive away. A Palace car was assigned for my use during my two-week stay in the kingdom. Ugyen, my long-time friend, was on hand to escort me to the Zhiwa Ling, a boutique hotel *very senior age of 92.*

*She often talked about explorers of old, many of whom had passed through her previous home in Kalimpong on the way in or out of Tibet. Such affinity for explorers was bestowed on me as well, though I am surprised the due respect a Royalty would give to an eclipsing and archaic "profession".*

*The buffet lunch was sumptuous, with a variety of appetizers and multiple main dishes, followed by desserts. Sitting next to Her Majesty, we continued our chat as she explained to me some of the dishes I had chosen. "This rice is special, grown in Bhutan, you must try" she articulated. I admired her graceful table setting, with the placemat set imprinted with a pagoda and flowers designed by Her Majesty.*

*At one point, our conversation turned to the Black-necked Crane, a stately bird living on the Tibetan Plateau, with some flocks wintering in Bhutan. It was through a poem by the 6th Dalai Lama mentioning this crane that the 7th reincarnation of the Dalai Lama was found. I tried to play smart and used the Tibetan name for the bird, "Chong Chong". Her Majesty corrected me right away. "It is Thrung Thrung, pronounced with a T," she said.*

*In passing, Her Majesty said, "it is unfortunate today that so many people are concerned only about making money." I quickly mentioned that it was not always the case, as there were certainly exceptions like the core supporters of CERS, many of whom were also successful businessmen, funding both our exploration and conservation efforts, including some in Bhutan.*

Lunch at Her Majesty's Palace / 於皇太后的皇宮用午餐

Gift from 13th Dalai / 十三世達賴喇嘛送的禮物

As we walked back to the main sitting room after lunch, Her Majesty explained some of her relics and antiques on the wall or set in special places. It was traditional protocol that no photography be allowed inside the palace, but Her Majesty kept telling me to take pictures of those items she introduced to me, including thangkas of deities, and a set of carved statues of eleven sages presented to her family long ago by the 13th Dalai Lama. She also asked me to translate scroll paintings with Chinese script on them. One piece very special to her is a Tashi Gomang, a pagoda with many door openings hiding different deities. It is a gift presented to her by her son the 4th King, for her 90th birthday.

At the sitting room, we sat next to each other under the portrait of Her Majesty's root guru, the Dilgo Khyentse Rinpoche, and two other portraits of HM's mother and grandmother. As our conversation continued, she found out that I did not have a booklet she had reprinted from a 1950s publication in China regarding the pilgrim monk Fa-Hsien of the 4th Century. She started recounting the story of the monk's journey to Sri Lanka seeking original sutras and included even minute details of some horrific encounters Fa-Hsien had when returning to China by the sea route. Quickly, she asked her attendant to bring over a copy as a gift to me.

While seated, Her Majesty held my hand with an old mala in her other hand. "This will be for you to keep," she said while passing the mala to me. She had saved it for me, having used it often for her morning and evening prayers. I had bought this mala from a monk at a sacred mountain in the Tibetan region and had offered it to Her Majesty previously. Now she was returning it to me, after using it for a while. I would leave it in the shrine room of Namseyling Palace.

90th birthday Tashi Gomang gift /
九十歲大壽禮物紮西戈芒佛塔

Leaving Her Majesty's Palace, I head straight for Namseyling, with a small entourage of Palace Bodyguards as my concierge. An army truck is dispatched bringing many supplies and even firewood to the small palace, as I will be staying there for the rest of my time in Thimphu. I have loads of luggage, as after Bhutan I will head for Myanmar and then Sabah in Malaysia. They have to be moved up very steep traditional ladder-like stairs to the upper main floor.

Upon entering the main floor, I am surprised that my bed is set up in the most sacred room of the palace, inside the shrine room, with a Buddha statue in the middle and an altar with a lit butter lamp and seven offering cups. I can only think in a most humble way that I am supposed to make my daily prayers in taking up such a special place.

The antechamber room has three day-bed seats covered with leopard pelts, with traditional windows looking out to the distant hills and the garden below. Here is where I make my work station during my stay. This small room has many thangka paintings on the wall, and is filled with carpets and three takin rugs on the floor, reminding me of the "Sheep with the Golden Fleece". Takin being Bhutan's national animal.

On the counters and end tables are framed photographs of the Royal Family. Among them, one is of the young 4th King warmly wrapping his arm around Rani Chuni Wangmo Dorji, his grandmother and the mother of the Royal Grandmother. There is also an old photo of a somewhat dilapidated Namseyling, taken before it was restored to become the home of Rani Chuni Wangmo Dorji. Perhaps the most valuable frame is one hung on the wall, a sketching of a Goddess deity, drawn by the Royal Grandmother in 1946 when she was a princess of 16, before marrying to the Third King in 1951. 1946 was also when the young Princess Kesang Dorji, as the signature depicts, joined her mother Rani and sister Ashi Tashi on a 17-day horseback journey to Lhasa.

Bed in shrine room / 皇宮神龕室內我的床

hm's workstation / HM 的工作站

Takin rugs / 羚牛毛毯

The full name of the palace is Namseyling Phuntshok Gaki Choling Palace, a name given by the Dilgo Khyentse Rinpoche. It means Dharma Palace of Wish Fulfilling Auspicious Happiness, and Rani Chuni Wangmo Dorji lived here until her old age. The place was decorated by her and remains the same to this day. There are many huge ox horns with engraved ornaments, ancient metal shields, old weapons including swords, a twin-barrel rifle, twin-legged gun rest, ammunition bag made from spotted leopard, even a flint lock gun. Rani must like rattan and bamboo crafts, as there are many such items. Of the many quaint hats hanging, my eyes are caught by a bamboo fisherman's hat common in Hong Kong, something that I still use occasionally.

Her Majesty with brother at her wedding /
皇太后和兄長於她的婚禮

Outside the house, a huge garden is filled with apple orchards and even a few persimmon and peach trees. Rani Chuni Wangmo Dorji planted many fruit trees and flowers in the garden herself. Prior to her time, Bhutan does not grow apple, so she & her husband Gongzim Sonam Tobgye Dorji brought them from overseas and introduced the fruit to the kingdom. Now apple can be found everywhere in the market, and they are just now ripe in the garden.

Soon after I settle in, Her Majesty sends over dinner cooked at her Royal Palace. From now on, my breakfast and dinner will be prepared by the

*Palace. With these specially prepared dishes are more gifts, this time in the form of two bottles of Vitamins, two bottles of eyedrops for my eyes, and several sheets of tablets. With each, Her Majesty had written by hand the dosage that I should follow and take. Such attention to details provides me with a warm feeling beyond description, something that money cannot buy.*

*In the evening, the Palace Guards in attention start a big log fire in the side of the palace. They were heating special stones to red hot, then putting them in a special partition inside a wooden tub filled with mountain spring water piped from the garden. I bathe myself in this most wonderful Bhutan Hot Stone Bath that I had only read of and dreamed about before. I recall earlier seeing two soldiers carrying the tub across the garden and thinking it looked like a coffin. Now that coffin is providing a most exquisite experience for my entire body.*

*Soaking my body and mind, I begin to revisit something I had read a long time ago. It is Mark Twain's famous fiction, "The Prince and the Pauper." With such a showering of gifts and invitations to stay at this Namseyling Palace, should I consider myself an honored guest or a squatter? That question can never be answered. As with my mother's teaching, "no taking if no giving." I would need to make a long list to deserve and fulfill what I have now taken.*

*Momentarily, I recalled an episode which has eclipsed my mind for fifty years. Since high school, I have engaged myself in drama, be they Cantonese opera, Gilbert & Sullivan operetta, and Chinese plays. While at the University of Wisconsin at River Falls in the early 1970s, I once acted as a beggar in the Threepenny Opera. Later on, I acted in a children's play with the Drama Department.*

*Land of the Dragon was written by Madge Miller, sister of Agatha Christie, regarding a Chinese tale. I had the lead role of a child prince and a little dragon was following me around. The fairy tale seems appropriately reenacting itself, in land of the Druk, albeit the Dragon Kingdom.*

*As with Bhutan's Gross National Happiness (GNH), Tashi Delek!*

HM with twin-barrel gun / HM 跟雙管步槍

南西嶺皇宮與不丹皇太后陛下

回頭看，當初的謹慎與猶豫，看來有些不成熟與沒來由。第一次受邀住到南西皇宮 (Namseyling) 時，我有些不知所措與困惑，感覺自己何德何能，豈能借住如此尊貴的皇室故居？南西嶺皇宮是今年九十二歲不丹皇太后的老母親住了好久的家。皇太后曾不只一次對我提議：「我希望你會喜歡南西嶺。」我一開始還懷疑自己是不是聽錯了，畢竟她說起話來總是輕聲細語，彷彿在你耳畔喃喃低語。

但每一次當我有機會在宮殿裡見到皇太后時，她總不厭其煩地反覆提醒。某次訪問不丹期間，太后陛下的孫女艾殊・吉桑 (Ashi Kesang) 公主，帶我兩度參觀南西嶺。這地方看起來就像個小型博物館，典藏許多歷史舊照與文物，是皇太后已故的母親拉尼・楚尼・旺姆・多傑 (Rani Chuni Wangmo Dorji) 的家。不過，從二十世紀七〇年代以來，這房子已無人居住，或許八〇年代期間，偶有人短暫住過。不然的話，那大概就只有神靈諸仙來借宿過了。艾殊・吉桑公主一再提及，對我的這份邀請，乃出於真心誠意，而非臨時起意或隨口說說。

自此，我開始認真思考，要如何以一種充滿敬意的方式來接受這份來自皇室的盛情邀約。我的母親從小就對我耳提面命：「你若無法反饋，就不要接受」，這句話已內化成我致力遵守的座右銘。我對「反饋」的定義是——不盡然要對施予者的特定對象給予回報，而是把回饋的對象，擴展至更廣義的「他者」。在這樣的情境下，我把「中國探險學會」當成一個取捨之間的渠道，從中建立了平衡的和諧之美。

八月二十九日，我從香港出發。在曼谷轉機停留一晚，我踏上隔天清晨七點的不丹皇家航空，出發前往不丹。飛機緩緩降落帕羅機場時，不斷以八字型曲折迴轉而下，穿越綠意盎然的山間景緻，對我來說，已不再是個毛骨悚然的驚詫，而是一次滿心期待的快樂兜風，因為我很欣賞機長平穩而準確無誤的駕馭自如。抵達機場後，雖然因應新冠疫情的快篩測試與填寫表格而花了些時間，不過，移民通關的過程快速而順利。

從機場到首都廷布 (Thimpu)，要大約一小時車程。我在不丹旅居的兩週期間，皇室特派了一台車讓我使用。我的老朋友烏顏 (Ugyen) 護送我到織瓦靈 (Zhiwa Ling) 飯店，這是一間蓋在廷布山區一片松樹林中的精緻飯店。

飯店自新冠疫情至今，已休館了兩年半，如今重新經營，我是重啟大門後的第一位客人。不過，嚴格說來，我不算第一位。在疫情最嚴峻期間，現任國王，亦即不丹第五任國王，不畏危急而到國內各地四處奔波，安撫百姓、鼓勵臣民；那段期間，國王偶爾會把這家飯店當成自我隔離的地方。聽說，國王去年待在家裡的

Rani Chuni Wangmo Dorji /
拉尼・楚尼・旺姆・多傑

Zhiwa Ling Hotel / 織瓦零飯店

時間只有四十三天。

抵達不丹隔天，皇太后邀請我九月一日到她的宮殿裡一起吃午餐。我其實早有準備，預料此行會見到皇太后，因為我是受她邀請來訪不丹，我的簽證也是以皇室貴賓身分簽發的。也因此，我才不必像一般觀光客那樣，必須支付「每日最低旅遊規費」；不過，其實在我離開後，不丹也尚未對遊客重新開放。

皇太后的宮殿離我住的飯店不遠，只需要五分鐘路程。我們在她的主客廳見面，她戴著一條色澤鮮艷的犛牛圍巾，那是較早以前我送她的禮物。這條圍巾印上我在西藏一座高山山口拍攝的經幡照。當我向她提及她身上的圍巾時，她告訴我圍巾美極了，她視如珍寶。從上一次見面至今已三年，皇太后看來似乎比過去消瘦了些。

一如歷史上各個朝代的使節向皇帝進貢珍稀物品，我為皇太后獻上少許禮物，但卻從我所敬愛的這位皇室密友手中，接受更多回贈的厚禮。皇太后送我的禮物以絲帶包裝得很精美，其中包括與不丹王國相關的大量歷史書籍，特別是對皇太后家族的內部事蹟。另外，還有幾瓶不同口味的自製果醬、一條編織厚毯、十八年的不丹威士忌、一盒月餅，和串了一百零八顆金琥珀色的瑪拉念珠。

Into Paro for landing / 降落帕羅機場

久別重逢的我們，一邊喝茶，一邊聊起上一次見面後的生活，親近無私，暢所欲言。因為疫情，我們已睽違三年。皇太后熱愛閱讀，是個狂熱的讀者，她多次向第四任國王推薦我的著作與定期書寫的通訊文，她告訴我，國王也喜歡閱讀我的探險經歷與故事。「在這個時代還能有你這樣的探險家，真是太驚訝了啊，黃博士。」皇太后每每重複這句感慨之言時，總會這樣尊稱我；幾乎每一次見面都會聽她如此肯定我，無一例外，現在又一次了。由此可見，皇太后對探索抱持高度興致，即使已高齡九十二，似乎仍不減她的熱情。

她經常會提及年代久遠的探險家，其中許多人都曾在出入西藏的途中經過她的老家──噶倫堡 (Kalimpong)。我也有幸被賦予這份同為探險家的肯定，確實令我受寵若驚，因為難得見到一位年邁的皇室成員會對一份過時又古老的「專業」，賦予應有的尊重。

午餐饗宴很豐盛，有各種開胃菜與主食，然後是甜點。坐在皇太后身邊，我們繼續暢所欲言，她看著我所挑選的食物，還特別為我說明介紹──「這種米很特別，是在不丹種的，你一定要嚐

Gifts from Her Majesty / 皇太后贈送的禮物
Her Majesty with HM & mala / 皇太后和 HM 還有瑪拉念珠

嗜。」她說起話來，清晰明白。我很欣賞她優雅的餐桌擺設，餐墊上印有皇太后親自設計的寶塔與花卉。

我們之間無所不談的對話，一度轉到黑頸鶴的話題，這是青藏高原上「莊嚴高貴」的候鳥，其中部分黑頸鶴會飛到不丹過冬。六世達賴喇嘛曾在一首詩裡提及，因為此鶴的牽引，才順利找到轉世的第七世達賴喇嘛。我想要耍小聰明，刻意在皇太后面前使用黑頸鶴的西藏語「衝衝」；隨即被皇太后糾正：「是『特魯翁』(*Thrung Thrung*)，母音是 *T*」。

陛下順帶一提，感慨道：「今天很多人有點可悲，一心只想要多賺錢。」我趕緊回應，事實不盡然如此，總有例外，至少我認識的許多「中國探險學會」的核心支持者，他們當中不乏成功商人，但卻慷慨解囊，支助我們的探勘工作與環境保護的各種計畫，其中也包括在不丹的工作。

午餐後，我們一起走到主客廳，皇太后向我解說掛在牆上或放置特殊角落的一些古物與古董。按照傳統禮節，在皇宮內是不

Namseyling before restoration / 南西嶺皇宮整修前
4th King with grandmother Rani Chuni Wangmo Dorji /
第四世國王和祖母拉尼‧楚尼‧旺姆‧多傑

(takin) 羚牛毛毯，讓我想起了「金毛羊」。而不丹國獸，正是「羊頭犛牛身」的「塔金」羚牛。

在長桌與桌角處，擺放了鑲框的皇室家族照片。其中一張是年輕的第四任國王熱情摟著外祖母——也就是皇太后的母親拉尼·楚尼·旺姆·多傑的手臂。還有一張是南西嶺皇宮的老照片，皇宮看起來有些破舊，應該是為皇太后的母親翻修前的舊樣貌。所有畫像中，或許最有價值的，是牆上一幅女神像的素描畫，那是皇太后在一九四六年的創作。一如素描照底下的簽名落款與日期，一九四六時的皇太后，還只是個十六歲的公主——格桑·多傑 (Kesang Dorji)，她就是在那一年和母親拉尼，以及姊姊阿什·扎西 (Ashi Tashi) 一起完成十七天的馬背上之旅——騎馬前往拉薩。年輕的皇太后，直到一九五一年才與第三任國王結婚。

南西嶺皇宮的全名是「*Namseyling Phuntshok Gaki Choling*」宮，由頂果欽哲仁波切賜名——意指這是「以願力成就吉祥與幸福」的宮殿，皇太后的老母親拉尼·楚尼·旺姆·多傑在此安居到晚年。主人把皇宮裝飾與照顧得極好，至今仍美輪美奐。這裡刻有許多巨大牛角的裝飾物、古老的金屬盾牌與舊式武器，包括利劍、雙管步槍、雙足槍托、斑點豹皮製作的彈藥袋與燧發槍。室內還有許多藤製與竹編文物，拉尼一定是對這類工藝品情有獨鍾。環顧四週，還可瞥見許多古意懷舊的帽子，我的目光被其中一頂香港常見的竹編漁夫帽所吸引，這是我至今仍偶爾會派上用場的帽子。

屋外是種滿果樹的大花園，除了蘋果樹，還有些柿子樹與桃樹。皇太后的母親拉尼·楚尼·旺姆·多傑，生前種下許多果樹與花卉。在此之前，不丹不曾有蘋果樹，最初

由她和丈夫 (Gongzim Sonam Tobgye Dorji) 從國外購入，也由他們首先把蘋果引進不丹。現在，市場上隨處可見蘋果，而花園裡的蘋果也正好成熟了。

安頓好之後，皇太后派人從皇宮送晚餐過來。從現在起，我的早餐和晚餐都將由皇宮替我準備。眼前除了這些特殊菜餚餐點，還有許多生活保健品，包括兩瓶維生素、兩瓶眼藥水和幾片藥。每一物件都有皇太后親手寫下該注意的服用劑量。如此體貼入微，令我心生難以言喻的溫暖，那是金錢買不到的真情實意。

傍晚時分，皇宮守衛在一旁搭起原木火堆；把特殊的石頭加熱到火急火燎，然後，滾燙的石頭移到木盆裡的特殊夾板，最後，從花園輸送來的山泉水再倒入木盆裡。我在大費周章又妙不可言的「不丹熱石浴」中享受泡湯澡——如此場景，我曾讀過，也曾夢過，如今親身體驗，卻恍如夢寐。我記得稍早時看到兩個士兵抬著浴缸穿過花園，我心裡還嘀咕那浴缸看起來真像一口棺材。真想不到，這口「棺材」竟為我提供最極致的身心享樂。

浸泡的身心逐漸沈澱，我重新回望很久以前讀過的著名小說，馬克吐溫的《王子與貧兒》(或譯《乞丐王子》)。面對自己在南西嶺皇宮備受恩寵的高規格禮遇，我開始思索，到底該把自己視為尊榮的貴賓或棲身的寄居者？或許，永遠沒有答案吧。一如母親

Her Majesty's drawing of Goddess deity when she was teenager /
皇太后在十幾歲時畫的女神像

Bhutan Hot Stone Bath / 不丹熱石浴

對我的教誨:「你若無法反饋,就不要接受」。看來,我需要列個長長清單,審視自己配得之處,和我當下已得之物。

頃刻間,我想起縈繞心中五十年、久久揮之不去的畫面。我從高中開始就熱衷戲劇,無論粵劇、吉爾伯特與蘇利文的「薩伏依歌劇」或中國話劇,無所不愛。七〇年代初期,我還在美國威斯康辛大學河布分校唸書時,還曾於「三便士歌劇」中扮演乞丐一角。我後來甚至在戲劇系的兒童劇中粉墨登場——那場兒童劇是根據偵探作家阿嘉莎·克莉絲蒂 (Agatha Christie) 的妹妹瑪吉·米勒 (Madge Miller) 所撰寫的《龍之地》(Land of the Dragon) 所改編,內容講述的是中國的故事,我擔綱男主角的小王子角色,後面還有一條跟進跟出的小龍。這則童話故事似乎也適合在這塊不丹國「竺域」(Druk) 上演,更何況,按此梵語之意,這裡正是「雷龍之國」呢!

僅此向不丹的國民幸福指數看齊——「扎西德勒」(Tashi Delek)——滿心祝福,吉祥好運!

HM with Aide-de-Camp / HM 和副官

不
丹
邊
境
與
其
他
（
上
）

# BHUTAN BORDER BARTER ET AL (Part I)

Laya, Bhutan – September 10, 2022

## BHUTAN BORDER BARTER ET AL (Part I)

### In search of Yeti and Yak

*Princess Ashi Kesang's mobile phone showed something quite impressive; "21373 steps, measuring 15.21 kilometers." Now that's not a short hike, especially at an elevation between 2330 to 3830 meters, though we are doing it in reverse, dropping in altitude by 1500 meters on our way back to "civilization." Topping it all, it was done within three hours.*

*In case my readers are concerned about my calories burnt and weight lost, worry not. Her phone was working alright but was counting every step of the horses that we were riding. Royal steps you may call them, as Ashi Kesang is a member of the Royal family (Ashi means "Lady"), and my horse Norchu, meaning "Younger Brother", and Nakhu, meaning "Black" were provided by the Fourth King of Bhutan.*

*Two stallions were chosen from His Majesty's royal stables, for my use on this week-long excursion to Laya, a region on the high plateau with four villages all within ten kilometers of the border with Tibet. A third horse, belonging to Laya's former village chief, was added on our return trip. Three soldiers, stable-keepers of the Royal Body Guard, were dispatched to care for the horses and as my escort.*

Norchu & Nakhu Royal stable keepers / 諾儲和納庫和皇家馬廏管理員

*I have had some relatively long rides over my exploration career, two of which involved nine days on horseback and, at other times, even riding yak-back. But this is the first time that I have had someone leading my horse full-time, with at least one and at times two guards by my side to make sure that I do not fall off the horse.*

*Norchu is a well-trained stallion and saddled with a fine leather "seat" with engraved gold-lined red padding. He measures up to the task, taking me carefully and steadily up and down a rather slippery trail over smoothed-out rocks and wet mud. Laya is our destination. I am hoping to have a date with the renowned Yeti of the Himalayas. If the Yeti should decline my invitation, getting to meet the yak herders will be my consolation prize.*

*Getting to the trail head during rainy season is no easy endeavor. It involves driving all day from Thimphu through Punakha to below Gasa Dzong and staying overnight at the Tshachu Hotspring. It is believed that 128 varieties of local medicine emerge from the spring. Alas, the pleasure of soaking myself like last time inside the private* royal bath (with permission from the 5th King) is no more. A huge flood carrying large boulders down the Mo Chhu River in August 2021 has washed off just about everything in sight; all the buildings, public or private, next to the river. In their place is a make-shift canvas tent, with a small temporary pool, for the few visitors who dare brave the hazards to return. I am one such rare and lonely soul who spends half an hour sitting in this medicinal spring.

Next morning, we drive past Gasa and head toward the trail head. The scenery, with haze and fog rising from the gorges, is gorgeous. Streams and waterfalls among flush forest punctuate the view. Almost two hours on rough dirt road, barely wide enough for one car, takes us to a gushing river with an army-built steel bridge. Right before the bridge is a huge active landslide, spanning perhaps a two hundred meters stretch of the road, with one side falling into the river below.

Flooded hot spring with tent / 溫泉被大水沖壞和臨時帳篷        HM in pool / HM 泡溫泉

Two backhoe machines are excavating in a futile attempt to clear the road as we arrive at the scene. Each dig starts triggering yet another small slide of earth from the side of the mountain. Over decades of exploration throughout the Tibetan plateau, I have often witnessed such road clearing during rainy season. And rainy season is still here with us in Bhutan, being on the south slope of the Himalayas, with even more precipitation falling.

My escort team, including two monks, panic for a while, as they cannot find me. They are looking in the wrong place, in the back, not knowing that I have walked to the hazardous front of the landslide to assess the situation and am taking some action photographs, a routine of any well-trained frontline journalist.

Momentarily the two earth-diggers stop their operation and move to the end of the slide to allow us to pass. Our driver engages the four-wheel-drive and rushes right through. As we hurry past the dug area, fresh earth and small rocks are still gushing down. After our two pick-up trucks have passed, the army truck carrying the two royal horses follows right behind.

Less than half an hour ahead and the road ends. Here a number of huts serve as temporary warehouses for the local villagers, filled with cases and bags of their goods and supplies to be loaded onto horses and mules before these caravans embark on the mountain trail to the villages beyond. We too, disembark here, waiting while the horses are untied from the army truck and prepared for the journey ahead. Around half a dozen mules are already waiting. They will become our personal caravan carrying everything we might require for the days to come inside the mountain.

The onward riding journey takes five hours. Some stretches are so narrow that only one person can gingerly pass.

*Riding on a horse through such an area can be a bit hair-raising. At one section, the fast river floods right up to the path, and my horseman has to take each step carefully while leading my horse. I hold my breathe until we are safely across. Several wooden bridges also span other tributary rivers or streams. In between some flush pine forest dripping with full-grown lichen, we stop for a picnic lunch, looking down onto a fast-running river below as we rise higher and higher in elevation.*

*Near the confluence of two rivers sits an army camp with a dozen or so soldiers. They are here to guard the border with Tibet, which is around ten kilometers away, beyond some high snow mountains and glaciers. Much of the northern border of Bhutan with China is quiet and safe, unlike further west near the tri-nation region of Yatung where part of China is sandwiched between India and Bhutan. I have had the good fortune to explore that area twice over the years.*

Waterfall on way to Laya / 前往拉雅村的瀑布

*The Yatung region, as a historical and traditional trade route between the north and south of the Himalayas, has seen a few tense and sensitive moments, not unlike the storms and avalanches seen by the formidable snow mountains. Remote as many of the border regions are, it is not surprising that there are well-defined borders and undefined borders, as well as disputed borders. Perhaps the last problem would be for more inspired and wiser future leaders of respective neighboring countries to solve, hopefully in an amicable way.*

*As I always point out, neighboring countries will not move away, whether you like them or not. You must reckon with them despite differences. It is always better to be friends than enemies, saving anxiety and resources. Others from distant lands are more likely to be fair-weather friends, disappearing once their self-interests are served. But because of internal or international politics, political sense often trumps common sense, and long-term interest gives way to short-sightedness.*

*It is with such thoughts in my mind that I ride closer and closer toward the border of Bhutan with China, feeling lucky and special that I should arrive as a Chinese, but from the Bhutanese side. Accompanied by a most helpful and attentive team of Bhutanese makes it even more special. How I wish I could reciprocate in the future and accompany my Bhutanese friends to visit the border from the Chinese side.*

Border army camp / 邊境軍營

被洪水破壞殆盡的現場，搭起臨時的帆布帳篷，蓋了個小型臨時水池，僅供少數勇於冒險前來的遊客，泡在水裡而聊以慰藉。我就是其中一個少見而孤獨的靈魂，恣意讓自己浸泡在此「不復當年」的水療溫泉裡，兀自坐了半小時。

隔天清晨，我們驅車經過加薩，朝著山路口前行。峽谷中的山霧彌漫，氤氳繚繞，景色迷人。山間叢林中的溪流與瀑布，更增添野地的美麗富饒。眼前的小徑，窄得容納不了一台車，我們就在這條崎嶇不平的泥路上行駛了將近兩小時，才抵達一條水流湍急的河流，橫越河上的，是座軍用鋼橋。鋼橋的正前方，是個巨大而蠢動的土石流滑坡，霸氣地橫跨路面兩百公尺長的道路，另一側山體則已落入下方水流中。

當我們抵達現場時，兩台挖土機已在孜孜不倦地挖掘，試著清理滿目瘡痍的道路，但似乎久攻不下，效果有限。每一次開始挖掘其中一個小山坡時，另一邊的山頭土堆，則蠢蠢欲動而危如累卵，似乎難以兼顧。在我數十年來的青藏高原探索中，我經常在雨季中目睹過類似的道路清理工程。今天，由於不丹位處喜馬拉雅山南邊坡地，降雨量較多，因此，不丹這一邊依舊風急雨驟。

我的守衛隊包括兩位僧侶，因為一轉身找不到我而慌張起來。其實，是他們找錯地方了，我不在他們後方，我因為評估了現狀而獨自走到山體滑坡那頭較危險的前端，想要到土石流前方拍些現場的照片，這是專業訓練的前線記者理所當然的職責。

兩台挖土機看到我們一行人出現，立即停止挖掘作業，轉移到土石堆後端，為我們騰出一條通道。我們的司機啟動四輪驅動，趕緊直衝過去。當我們倉促跨越挖土區域時，

Gasa gorges / 加薩峽谷

新舊大小石塊仍不斷滾落而下。兩台皮卡車通過後，接著是運載兩匹皇家馬的軍用卡車，緊隨在後。

往前行不到半小時，已是道路盡頭。這裡為當地村民蓋了不少臨時倉房，規模不大，裡面裝滿一箱箱已經打包好的貨品，等馬與騾所組成的「物流」商隊準備往山路出發時，就可以把這些物品運往其他村莊。我們在這裡停靠，等待我們的馬匹從軍用卡車解下，期待「馬到」功成，凜凜前行。大約有六隻騾馬已在一旁整裝待發。這群騾馬是我們的私人商隊，我們未來幾天在山裡所需要的民生用品，都放到騾子上，由牠們負責運送。

我們這段騎行的旅程，歷時五個小時。有些路段極其狹窄，騎著馬經過這些僅容一人「輕身」通過的區域，何止如履薄冰，簡直險象環生得令人頭皮發麻。我們甚至經過一個急流小河直接淹沒的路段，我的騎手牽馬走過時，邁出的每一步都必須小心翼翼。我下意識地斂聲屏息，等著整個團隊安然渡過後才放心大口喘氣。過程中也跨越幾座木橋，橋下是其他支流的大小溪河。我們在一塊長滿苔蘚地衣的松樹林間，停留憩息，吃頓野餐，邊吃邊

Working on landslide / 清理土石流
Army truck with horses / 軍用卡車載馬
Bridge crossing / 過橋

凝視下方湍急流淌的水流，可想而知，我們已步步登高，置身海拔更高處了。

兩條河流的交匯處，有個軍營，裡面有十幾位士兵在此駐紮，守護邊界。這裡距離西藏邊境只有大約十公里之遙，隔著大雪山與冰川。不丹北方與中國邊界的大部分區域，相對平靜安全，不像西部地區與亞東三國的邊境週遭——過去幾年來，我有幸曾兩度探索該地，了解當地因中國部分區域夾在印度與不丹之間，而難免齟齬於其中，進而橫生枝節。

身為喜馬拉雅山南北縱線的歷史與傳統貿易路線，亞東區域那股暗潮洶湧的張力，從來沒有少過，和大雪山所瞥見的風暴與雪崩不相上下。由於許多邊境地處偏遠，國與國之間的邊界至今仍存在一些明確與模糊之間、各自表述的爭議之處，長久以來，這樣的角力與敏感關係，已見怪不怪。或許，最後的議題終將由個別的鄰國推派更有魄力與智慧的未來領袖來解決，但願是以友善和平的方式來解決。

一如我向來的立場，無論你喜不喜歡，身邊的鄰國都不會搬離。儘管彼此的嫌隙分歧依舊在，你還是得面對與處理。做朋友總比樹敵好，省得焦慮緊張又浪費資源。至於一些看似比較大公無私的遠方友人，或許就在滿足自身利益之後便銷聲匿跡了。話說回來，自家國內與國際間的交鋒所衍生的政治意識，往往戰勝理性的常識，因此，長期利益經常得在短視近利的盲點下，被輕易犧牲了。

我心懷這份思維，騎馬朝向不丹與中國的邊界，越騎越近時，心中竟為自己能以中國人的身分，從不丹這一頭奔往邊界疆域，而備覺榮幸。再環顧四週這群陪伴在側的不丹人團隊，他們的緩急相助與無微不至，就更別具意義了。我多麼希望自己未來也能如此善待與回報我的這群不丹朋友，陪伴他們從中國那一頭，走向兩國的邊境之地。

不
丹
邊
界
與
其
他
（
下
）

# BHUTAN BORDER BARTER ET AL (Part II)

Laya, Bhutan – September 10, 2022

Ashi with Kenley on right /
艾殊・格桑公主在肯利右側
Pem with black curly hair / 芃黝黑的捲髮

in elevation, the fireside is a most welcome place in the evening and here becomes our floor dining circle. Even the cat refuses to leave the room and sleeps on my lap by the fire. And it is rare that a simple bowl of noodles with two tiny sausages tastes so good. Perhaps after five hours on horseback it is not so odd.

Outside the home, Kenley runs the show, like caravan and trading. But once passed the door, Pem has all the say. At one point, we ask Kenley why he does not start the fire, and he tells us that, until his wife says so, he cannot do so. Once when Pem is away with other neighborhood ladies to do a day-long session of praying, we ask Kenley whether he can show us the family's valuable cordyceps fugus. He draws a blank, saying he knows nothing about where anything is kept. Precise division of power and labor obviously keeps the household peaceful.

I fancy the jet black and curls of Pem's hair, offering that she must have it dyed. Not so; they are all natural. I wonder if she was using the cordyceps before the "caterpillar fungus" became the most-prized income for those living on the high plateau. I finally get to see these fortune-makers. Pem shows me various grades from three different regions nearby, each looking quite different, and thus priced differently. The best kind, called Super A, can fetch 2,800,000 Nu (one USD equals 80 Nu) for one kilo, whereas the

Houses of Laya / 拉雅的房屋

cheapest goes for only 200,000 Nu per kilo.  Everyone confirms that cordyceps yield has decreased a lot, and they feel that it has been affected by climate change.  Ultimately, through Monk Sonam who accompanies us, I will purchase a kilo of the cheapest ones to take home.

Ashi has prepared various gifts on our behalf to give to each of the people who are involved in accommodating or serving us. Suddenly, Pem utters two Chinese words, "ganxie" meaning "thank you".  To reciprocate, Pem gives me seventeen very fine and pretty cordyceps.  They come to show the generosity of these remote and earthy people.

Following on her two Chinese words, I ask Pem about the very large and heavy old model Changhong television in our room; how and where they acquired it.  It turns out that the couple has been across the border three times over the years and has gone all the way to Lhasa for pilgrimage during winter months.  The last visit was twenty years ago.  After walking two days, including crossing the border at Nyero and the pass Waki La near Phari, they would catch a car ride by the road to Lhasa.  They would do this at night so few questions were asked.

For Bhutanese here, they still cross into Tibet to go on pilgrimage while doing some trading and purchasing.  Cordyceps is of course the main cash crop, whereas to bring back, they might purchase all kinds of daily utensils, clothes, even items as large as a TV and small items like pink rock salt.  Today, sea salt substitutes for that from Tibet.  All business is done through bartering with locals.  For the Tibetans crossing into Bhutan however, it is quite a different matter.  Twenty years ago, many Tibetans crossed the border to pick cordyceps on the Bhutanese side.  Chased away by

Bhutanese soldiers, they would return the very next day. This intrusion was not stopped until Bhutan raised the issue to the Chinese government. From then on, the Chinese have tightened their border control and no more penetration happens.

I have requested a chance to talk to a local who claims to have seen a Yeti. Lopen Kenchog (64) shows up from Loopcha, the nearest neighbouring village with some twenty families. Lopen and his younger brother together have married the same wife; not an unusual practice in remote regions of the plateau and practiced to this day even in Tibet. This is the traditional way to keep family fortune and livestock under the same roof, and it seems to have stood the test of time. Lopen is the local fourth-generation clergyman with special ability to connect to deities, like a shaman who can get possessed by spirits and reach out to the supernatural. Lopen began being possessed at the age of ten. He seems a natural storyteller and begins a sermon on his various unusual encounters, illustrated with many facial and hand expressions.

Answering my interest about the Yeti, his version is quite unlike the legendary abdominal snowman or that described within Tin Tin in Tibet. Instead, they march in small group through the thick of the forest like little dwarfs. No huge footprints in the snow nor hairy beast pounding his chest

Ashi & HM / 艾殊・格桑公主和 HM
Lopen storytelling clergy /
羅彭和尚也是説書高手

like King Kong, but they are known to give out a whistling sound when alarmed. There are always more reports of Yeti sightings during the 8th and 9th month in the Bhutanese calendar, coinciding with the time of the migration for yak herding. The larger type of Yeti is human-sized, yet with a more protruded and pointed mouth. Lopen claims to have met one, a mega-Yeti, twenty-one years ago. At times, entire group of herders will claim to have seen one together, giving credence to the story.

Lopen provides far more detailed and dramatic descriptions of another strange animal he has encountered, something hairy and looking like a donkey. The feet are like those of a bear and it can hug and climb a tree. Its spine and face are white with shorter hair, and it roars like a donkey. Locals call it "chhurail" and it is featured in sculptures at the foot of the Buddha. For us, it is the legendary Qilin, or Kirin in Japanese, a sacred and mythical animal used as brand name for a popular beer from Japan.

By the third day, one of our accompanying monks, Kencho Gyaltshen, is complaining about losing sleep for two nights. His home is near Gasa and he has been the head monk of the Antiquities Department in Thimphu that Ashi runs as a culture conservation effort. It turns out that, with a lack of coffee to numb his head, he cannot intoxicate himself to an extent that he is knocked out and goes to sleep. This is the most strange malady of insomnia I have ever come across. Meanwhile I worry, too, that my snoring will disturb Ashi sleeping in the next room.

On the third morning, our two horses are ready and one additional horse with a colorful saddle is prepared by the old chief for Ashi so we can head up high into the yak herding area. The young chief will accompany us, but refuses to ride, noting that he has too much compassion for the horses. I would feel humbled, had it not been I am into my seventh decade in age.

As we reach over 4000 meters and a small alpine lake, we run into our first yak herder. A lady is just finishing milking her yaks and I stop to take some photos before continuing. Within another fifteen minutes and higher still, we stop by a black yak hair tent. Riachen Sita (40) is the woman in charge here since she does most of the work regarding her yak herd, numbering forty including five bulls and eight calves born this spring.

She tells me that she milks her yaks only once a day, turning the milk into soft cheese, hard cheese and butter every two days. Most products the family will consume themselves, selling only a little to others. She even demonstrates how she churns milk into butter in a long cylinder made of a hollowed birch tree trunk. As with her yak hair tent, no one makes those anymore. Her tent was woven by her mother and has been in use for almost twenty years. She started tending to livestock even before that, at age 15. Her mother had eight kids, and now she has one son and one daughter.

Within her immediate area, there are half a dozen herders, each being allocated grazing grounds. Thus there is no dispute. Others drive their animals to farther and higher pastures. Where we are is her autumn pasture, whereas summer grazing ground is up still higher. Thus, she has to make four moves a year up and down the mountain. Higher up there are cordyceps, but each year the harvest becomes less, as the climate is getting warmer and the snowline moving higher.

*Beyond Riachen's camp, we ride higher still, arriving at a ledge overlooking the river and a confluence far below. Here at 4105 meters in elevation we stop for a picnic lunch and enjoy the cool mountain breeze, observing the coming and going of clouds. At this point my Galileo map shows that we are less than nine kilometers from the border with Tibet. Just before lunch, a total of thirteen of us put our hands to setting up a long string of prayer flags we have brought along all the way from Thimphu.*

*Back to Laya. I stop by a local school and am pleased to see the young students, all dressed in local costume, studying in the simple classrooms. As the next day is another rest day for us before heading back down the hill, we spend time looking at some of the crafts hand-made by the lady of our house. Pem has many woolen costumes and skirts, and we want to collect some as cultural artifacts to be left in Thimphu. Packed away nicely, they include two sets of full costume, two bamboo-woven hats for women, and two pairs of leather boots, one for a man and the other for a woman. These are the best trophies to take home.*

Riachen & yak tent / 萊雅辰和犛牛帳篷

Chat under prayer flags / 經幡下聊天

School in Laya / 拉雅的學校

*I have been hoping that we would run into a mild snow fall for me to capture some nice photographs. Heaven seems to have heard me and on the last night it snows a bit, just enough to give the high mountains a sprinkling of white to decorate my final pictures of Laya. As I finish our last ride on horseback and move to the cars before we drive away, two successive rainbows escort our departure. Each remains for almost half an hour as we drive past the gorges and flush valleys of Gasa. When we pass through the final gate from Gasa into Punakha Dzong, a third rainbow appears as if to welcome us. What an auspicious way it is to end a most wonderful journey!*

*Om Mani Padme Hum! Tashi Delek!*

Laya snow peaks / 拉雅的雪峰

不丹邊界與其他（下）

海拔高度 3830 公尺的拉雅高原，和不丹與中國邊境的直線距離，不到十二公里。這座高原是當地最大的部落社區，也是通往附近其他四個村落的交叉口，總人口將近三百戶人家。每一隊背負超過六、七隻家畜騾馬經過拉雅高原，一整天馬不停蹄地奔忙來去。牠們不只運載物資貨品，還運送大量建材物料，因為當地有不少興建中的新房屋與社區公共設施。雨季與收成的農忙都將告一段落了，正是大興土木的好時機。

木料是不丹的傳統房屋不可或缺的主要建材，這裡的大部分木材取自社區的森林，而大片公共林區也都設有妥善的保護措施。以喜馬拉雅山以南的國家來說，不丹對綠化與林木培植的重視與用心，是數一數二的好。不丹的面積比比利時或台灣還大，總人口略高於七十萬上下，相對而言，幾乎只有比利時十五分之一的人口，以及台灣三十分之一的人口。由此可見，不丹在保護土地的能力與決心，一如他們對傳統文化的保存，盡心竭力，且成效卓著。

七十二歲的老村長肯利・多傑 (Kenley Dorji) 與其妻，六十八歲的芃 (Pem) 女士，在進入拉雅高原之前的一片空地上，蓋了間非常寬敞的房子，窗明几淨。這個地方將成為我們接下來四晚的臨時住處。村長的兒子，四十一歲的古布・哲旺 (Gup Tshewang) 正在路上，趕來與我們會面。古布・哲旺最近在總計 267 戶的區域選舉中，獲選為拉雅高原

Passing caravan / 經過的商隊
Laya Village / 拉雅村庄
Route map of Laya Tibet border / 拉雅和西藏邊境的地圖路線

的新村長，同時也兼任加薩宗的副首長；值得一提的是，這群選民中，光是十八歲以上的選民就佔了大約七百名之多。自二○○八年以來，政府所提供的移動式服務已擴及拉雅高原，第四任與第五任國王都曾深入該區訪視，尤其年輕的第五任國王在新冠疫情前才剛到過拉雅高原。

我受邀到樓上的經堂房休息，但我決定婉拒這番好意，我心想如此神聖好房應當保留給格桑公主，她陪著我們到這裡來；我到隔壁的房間即可。我們在室內各個角落鋪上地毯，接下來幾天，這裡就是我們生活起居的窩了。

安頓好之後，我們隨即到樓下一間堆放木頭火爐的房裡，大夥兒圍繞著席地而坐，開始輕鬆閒聊。在這海拔 4000 公尺的高原上，尤其冷颼颼的夜晚，溫熱的火源，人人趨之若鶩，恨不得湊近取暖，頓時也就成了我們圍繞著進食的「地板餐桌」。就連貓咪也不肯離開溫暖的房間，就近火爐邊，懶洋洋地窩在我的大腿上，闔眼安眠。手上一碗再尋常不過的湯麵配上兩根小香腸，竟然如

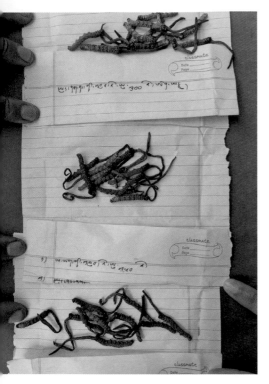

Cordyceps from various places /
來自各地的冬蟲夏草

此美味,實在少見。或許在馬背上行進了五小時後,看似簡簡單單的溫熱與暖胃,都成了最銷魂的享樂。

這個家,典型男主外、女主內。家門以外的所有行動調度,譬如馬隊與買賣交易等,由老村長肯利當家作主;可一旦進了家門內,一切老婆說了算。芃女士的權勢不可小覷,某天我們好奇探問老村長何以天冷不起火,他告訴我們,沒有老婆恩准,他可不敢「輕舉妄動」。有一次老婆大人和鄰居姐妹們外出一整天去祈禱誦經,我們問肯利,能不能讓我們瞧瞧家裡珍藏、價值連城的冬蟲夏草。肯利一臉迷惘困惑,聲稱到底哪些東西擺放哪個角落,他一無所知。看來,明確的權利義務與精準的分工合作,是這個家庭始終維持寧靜祥和的主要因素。

我猜想女主人的捲曲黑髮肯定是染黑的。不過,事實不然,這一頭黑捲髮沒有一絲「人為加工」,完全天然。那我就更好奇了,我猜想女主人是不是在「毛毛蟲菌種」的冬蟲夏草一夕成名而成為高原子民最豐厚的收入之前,她就已大量服用冬蟲夏草,才蓄得這一頭烏黑美髮。拐彎抹角的猜測促狹一輪後,我終於如願以償,親眼看見這些財富之源。女主人芃女士向我展示源自附近三個不同區域的品種,每一種看起來都各不相同,價格也天差地遠。最優質的一種是超級 A,一公斤要價 280 萬努 (1 美金兌換 80 努 ),而最便宜的品種,每公斤單價是 20 萬努。我所遇過的每一人都肯定地告訴我，冬蟲夏草的產量下跌很多，直指背後主因是氣候變遷的影響。我後來透過一路陪同我們的索南 (Sonam) 和尚居間溝通，我告訴他們自己要購買一公斤的冬蟲夏草，品種一般即可。

其實，艾殊公主早已貼心代我們預備了各種禮物，要送給每一位接待或服務我們的對象。出乎意料之外，女主人芃女士的口中突然說出兩個中文字「感謝」；她竟出於回報而把十七跟非常優質與漂亮的冬蟲夏草送給了我。他們向我們這群外來客旅展示了來自偏遠樸實子民的慷慨與好客。

話匣子一開，我隨口和女主人聊起房間裡那台又大又重的舊款長虹電視，我對這台電視的身世背景，深感好奇。原來，這對夫妻多年來已曾跨越國界三次，在冬季時從不丹前往西藏拉薩朝聖。最後一次去拉薩已是二十年前的事。當時，夫妻倆徒步走了兩天兩夜，途中跨越了尼羅 (Nyero) 與鄰近帕里 (Phari) 的瓦基拉山口，然後，在路邊攔了部車子，便一路顛簸到拉薩。夫妻倆選擇在夜間上路，所以一路幾乎很少面臨任何刁難的盤查。

Laya woman / 拉雅婦人　　　　　　　　　　Monk Sonam & cat / 索南和尚和貓

對許多不丹人來說，跨越國界到西藏，不僅為了朝聖，也希望能順道做些生意與交易。當然，冬蟲夏草是他們主要可以變現的經濟作物，出售手中的珍惜物品，換購的可能是各種日常用具、衣物、甚至包括「重大物品」如一台電視，也有輕巧小物如粉紅岩鹽。今天，海鹽已取代西藏鹽。這些所有採購與買賣都是與當地人面對面實際交易、討價還價而完成的。不過，對於進入不丹的西藏人來說，狀況則迥然不同。二十年前，許多西藏人跨越邊境到不丹採擷冬蟲夏草，但不丹士兵把這群外來的西藏人強行趕走，只是，隔天他們又回來了。一直到不丹向中國政府嚴正提出抗議後，自此，中國加緊邊界防守，非法越境的事才受到制止。

我提出心中期待，希望有機會與一位聲稱見過雪人的當地居民談談。六十四歲的羅彭‧肯措 (Lopen Kenchog)，來自一個大約只有二十幾戶人家的鄰近村莊盧普查 (Loopcha)。羅彭和他弟弟娶了同一個女性為妻，這在當地的偏遠高原區域並非什麼太罕見的事，即使在西藏也是常有的社會現象。對這樣的家庭來說，這是一個確保家庭財富與牲畜「不外流」的傳統方式，而這樣的家庭結構，似乎也經得起時間考驗而持守至今。羅彭是當地的第四代神職人員，天賦某種特殊神力，能與神明打交道，一如薩滿教的隱士般，能被神靈附體而進入「人神」狀態；他十歲時便已開始被神靈附身，掌握許多超自然的靈界本領。羅彭也是個與生俱來的說書高手，能言善道，說起各種超乎尋常的際遇時，豐富的臉部表情與手勢，有聲有色，引人入勝。

當我提起有關喜瑪拉雅雪人的興趣時，羅彭的回覆似乎與傳說中想像的奇特雪人大異其趣，也不像《丁丁在西藏》這本歷險記中所描繪的雪人。在他的敘述裡，這群雪人身型有如小矮人，成群結隊在森林深處遊走。雪地上從不曾出現任何巨大的腳印，也不是什麼毛茸茸的大野獸或動不動就搥打胸膛的大金剛猩猩；但據悉，這群小雪人只會在緊急時刻才會發出吹哨般的聲音。有趣的是，在不丹日曆的第八與第九個月的描繪中，可以找到更多與雪人相關的報告，恰好和犛牛的放牧與遷移時間，不謀而合。較大型的雪人身型，與一般人類大小無異，只是下巴嘴形更外凸。羅彭說，他在二十一年前曾遇過巨霸雪人。有些時候，當一群牧民異口同聲宣稱他們看到雪人時，更增添雪人故事的說服力與可靠性。

除了雪人之外，羅彭還告訴我們他曾遇過的另一種特殊動物，聽他繪聲繪影的形容與詳細說明，似乎是隻毛茸茸、看似驢子的動物。此物腳如熊，白色的背脊和臉，毛髮較短，叫聲像驢，可以抱樹、爬樹。當地人稱牠為「畜籟」(chhurail)，曾在佛祖的雕塑中出現，俯伏於佛祖腳下。在我們看來，所謂「畜籟」其實就是中國傳說與日語中被喻為神獸的「麒麟」，這名稱也是眾所週知的日本啤酒品牌。

第三天，其中一位隨行的和尚肯措・堅參 (Kencho Gyaltshen) 提起自己連續兩晚夜不成眠。堅參和尚協助艾殊公主在不丹首都廷布經營的文化保護事業，他在古物保存部擔任主責僧人；他的老家就在加薩附近。釐清失眠真相後，我才知道造成堅參失眠的罪魁禍首，是因為沒咖啡可喝；咖啡因對他不是醒腦而是陶醉，沒有咖啡，只能眾人皆睡他獨醒。我從未見過如此奇特的失眠理由。不過，我的夜夜好眠倒是讓我開始有些擔心了，不曉得自己的如雷鼾聲是否驚擾了隔壁房的艾殊公主？

第三天上午，我們的兩匹馬準備就緒，另外一匹馬是老村長為艾殊公主準備的，馬背上搭了個亮麗的彩色馬鞍，這麼一來，我們便可出發，往更高處的犛牛放牧區。年輕的村長一路陪同，但他拒絕騎馬，他說自己對馬有種特別的憐恤之情，捨不得騎。聽他這麼一說，我若不是七十高齡，肯定會覺得慚愧自責。

Monk Kencho with local / 肯措和尚與當地人

Milking yak / 擠犛牛奶

當我們抵達四千多公尺高原時，眼前有個小型高山湖泊，我們在此遇見當地第一位犛牛牧民。一位女士剛完成母犛牛的擠奶工作，我停下來拍了幾張照，然後再繼續前行。又過十五分鐘，我們已往更高處前行，在一個黑色犛牛毛的帳篷前，駐足停留。四十歲的萊雅辰・希妲 (Riachen Sita) 女士，是這個牧區的負責人，她一肩扛起總計四十頭犛牛群的放牧工作，包括五隻公牛和今年春天剛出生的八頭小牛犢。

希妲告訴我，她每天只給犛牛擠一次奶，集了兩天的奶量，把奶製成奶酪、硬質奶酪與奶油。大部分產品自給自足，只留下少部分出售。希妲甚至在我面前示範，看她如何在一個挖空的樺木長型圓筒中，把牛奶攪拌成奶油。回頭看她用犛牛毛織成的帳篷，現在的牧民已不再做這種帳篷了。希妲的這組舊帳篷是母親親手編織的，已經用了將近二十年。掐指一算，希妲在帳篷織好之前，大概十五歲左右吧，她便已學習照料牲畜，展開她的放牧人生。希妲的母親有八個孩子，而她現在也自己當媽了，育有一兒一女。

在她附近的區域，共有六家牧民，每一戶人家都被分配屬於自己的放牧區，牧者有其地，則可免除不必要的爭議。至於沒有放牧區的牧民，則把他們的牲畜趕到更遠更高的牧場去。我們置身之處，正是希妲的秋季牧場，她的夏季牧場在更高的高原上。也因此，隨著季節遞嬗，她每一年要山上山下移動四次，按季節更換牧場。在當地海拔更高處，有冬蟲夏草可採收，但由於整體氣候越來越暖和，雪線也隨之向更高海拔推進。

離開希妲的帳篷區，我們往高處騎行，抵達一座岩石突出的山壁前，往下可以俯瞰河流與水文匯流。這裡是海拔 4105 公尺高地，我們下馬暫歇，休憩野餐，一邊享受山風

Learning architecture design / 學習建築設計
Artifacts collected / 收集的文物

Punakha Dzong / 普納卡宗

輕拂的舒爽涼意，觀察千姿百態的雲層，在我們眼前來去自如。根據我的伽利略地圖顯示，我們離西藏的邊界不到九公里。剛剛午餐前，我們一行十三人還邊走邊手握一長串從廷布一路帶來的經幡旗幟掛到高高的長杆上呢！想不到西藏已近在眼前。

返回拉雅高原。我在當地一所學校前駐足停留時，瞥見一群身穿傳統服裝的年輕學子，在樸質簡陋的教室裡上課學習，我心中備感欣慰。由於隔天是休息日，因此，我們決定花些時間觀賞女主人芃女士親手製作的一些工藝品。女主人有不少羊毛服裝與裙子，我們搜集了一些衣物，準備放在首都廷布，作為文化藝術品的展示。我們小心翼翼把這些衣物包裝好，其中包括兩套完整的服裝，兩頂女士專用的竹編帽，以及男女皮靴各一雙。這是我們帶回去的最佳戰利品。

我一心期待能和一場溫和靜謐的降雪不期而遇，好讓我能從容不迫地拍幾張雪花飄零的浪漫美照。老天應該是聽到我的祈禱吧，在這裡的最後一晚，開始飄雪，正好為遠處高山蓋上白皚皚的山帽，讓我最後幾張拉雅高原的照片，終於多了白色雪花來點綴。騎馬行旅的最後一段，我們緩緩騎到車子停放區；大夥兒正準備開車離開前，天邊兩道延綿的絢麗彩虹，彷彿與我們一行人道別。驅車經過加薩水流湍急的峽谷時，兩道彩虹好似輪番上陣，各自停留空中將近半小時，護送我們離開。奇妙的是，當我們經過加薩的最後一道門、進入普納卡宗時，眼前竟又出現第三道彩虹，這回應該是為了歡迎我們吧！老天實在善待我們，在我們結束一段旅程時，恩賜我們如此炫目迷人又充滿好兆頭的奇景，豈不妙哉？

唵麼抳鉢訥銘吽！吉祥如意！

不丹女飛官

# FEMALE PILOT/CAPTAIN OF BHUTAN

Thimphu, Bhutan – September 14, 2022

*FEMALE PILOT/CAPTAIN OF BHUTAN*

*The flight into Bhutan is infamously frightful, drawing the breath away, especially for the faint-hearted.  Kids who love roller coaster rides, however, might enjoy the thrill, finding it awesome.*

*If you considered the last 90-degrees turn to land at old Kai Tak airport in Hong Kong tricky, try the figure 8, to be precise a "distraught figure 8ish pattern", needed to negotiate and bring a large plane through a series of mountain-lined switch-backs to land at Paro Airport.  Though listed as the third most difficult airport at which to land, the other two are only for small fixed-wing or STOL (short takeoff and landing) propeller planes, whereas Paro is for full-size Airbus jets.*

*Figure 8 is not just a figure of speech; it is usually used as flight pattern training for a drone or in figure skating, but not for a real airplane, unless you are piloting a fighter jet during a dogfight. And the danger is real. In 2004, my friend, the late David Tang, with a group of friends in a private jet flew into Bhutan for his 50th birthday.  During landing, the wing touched the ground, and the plane was appropriately grounded thereafter.  Judith, my dear friend from New York canceled her planned trip to Bhutan, when she found out that the captain of her private jet had to go through additional training in India before being allowed to fly into Paro Airport in Bhutan.*

Captain Ugyen handling controls / 機長尤茜掌控飛機
Switches of the overhead panel / 機長上方的操控儀表
HM selfie flying in cockpit / HM 於駕駛艙內自拍

*So, it is with many preconceptions that I sat down to talk to Captain Ugyen in Thimphu, the capital of the kingdom. By then I had made several visits to this wonderland and conducted some small projects in the country at the invitation of the Royal Grandmother, besides being received by that most senior member of the Royal Family.*

*Captain Ugyen came to meet me in her full regalia, hat, uniform and all, with four stripes on her shoulders. She is the first woman captain of Druk Air, the flag carrier of Bhutan and for a long time the only airline to serve the Himalayan kingdom; the only airline that dared serve this hazardous route, requiring precision as well as guts.*

*Captain Ugyen, however, does not look so gutsy; not macho at all, in fact. Her story went back twenty years. In 2003, Ugyen was finishing high school and heard that Drukair, the national airline of Bhutan, was short of pilots. She was curious and decided to check out the opportunity. But at the time Druk Air only provided one full and one half scholarship to two men, none to women, to go abroad and receive flight training. Still, she met Bhutanese Captain Chodea in 2004 and was encouraged to pursue her flying career. Later on, Captain Chodea also became her trainer when she*

Paro Airport / 帕羅機場
Terrain into Paro from the air /
空中看帕羅機場地形

joined Druk Air.

Ugyen successfully convinced her family to help support her to go to flight school, which was quite expensive. In January 2005, she went abroad and started her training. Of twenty plus students, there were only three or four women. After a year and eight month, she earned her wings as a commercial pilot and later met minimum hour requirements.

In 2007, she joined Drukair and began her line training in flight and, in over a year, became full-fledged First Officer in May of 2009. She flew for ten more years, logging 7,000 hours, before finally being promoted and being checked-out as Captain for the airline in 2018. As of today, 2022, she has logged over 8,000 hours in flight.

Today, even the senior pilots are only in their 50s and there are few chances for promotion for junior officers. However, the gender ratio has changed from when she first joined. With seven Captains in total and herself being the only female when she began, now there are four women within the full line-up of pilots.

That ratio is still small compared to many outside countries. Ugyen conveyed to me that there seem to be many more female pilots in India;

*while in flight, she can hear a lot more radio conversations with female voices. A sexist may say that is because women converse more. But in reality, India is a country with over twelve percent female pilots, more than twice the global average.*

*Flying into Bhutan is not the usual flying. Due to the difficult terrain and the Category C runway, there is absolutely no night landing. It is also a VFR (visual flight rules) operation airport. All Airbus aircraft were designed for a 45-meter wide runway for landing and take-off. But Paro Airport has only a 30-meter wide strip. The wingspan of the A320-neo, with 140 passengers maximum, that Captain Ugyen flies is over 35 meters, stretching beyond the runway's width. The length of runway being 2,265 meters, it is also barely long enough for takeoff. Furthermore, it sits at 2,244 meters in elevation. At such an altitude, the thinner air also provides less lift for the airplane when compared to sea level.*

*Despite that, Boeing sent a 737-700 to Paro and completed eleven successful test flights soon after the airstrip was completed. Nevertheless, Druk Air ultimately opted to use the Airbus 319 and 320 series. This may become more the norm than exceptions in the future, even for huge orders from countries like China. The Ukraine war has demonstrated that the long arm of US sanctions knows no borders. Potential buyers might worry about the honoring of purchase contracts and the risk of obtaining parts and maintenance should the government go berserk or get irrational based on external or internal political needs.*

*During the last two years of the pandemic, Captain Ugyen has flown many relief and Medevac flights, carrying emergency supplies or evacuating gravely ill Bhutanese back home for treatment when India found their own medical facilities overwhelmed. One of our own CERS directors quietly purchased and supplied much-needed*

Landing with wingspan over airstrip / 機翼寬度超過降落跑道
Last banking to level with runway / 調整與跑到齊平

A320n coming in to land at Paro /
空巴 A320n 準備降落帕羅機場

*pandemic equipment and had them flown into Bhutan. Captain Ugyen may possibly have piloted that flight.*

*During those heady days, she was required to enter into quarantine after each flight, either for twenty-one days in early 2020 or for two weeks later on. She did 21-days twice and has totally lost count of how many 14-days quarantine periods she had gone through within the past two years before it was finally reduced to 7-days earlier this year. Such dedication to a tough career during such a stressful time deserves another half a bar on her shoulder, if not a full bar.*

*At least two films of Captain Ugyen piloting, or should I say gracefully maneuvering, an Airbus into Paro Airport have been posted on YouTube. The best is a seven-minute plus version from June this year, with over 1.7 million viewers recorded so far and almost a thousand comments left. The style and relaxation with which she took this big bird down is what amazed many pilots, or wannabes still flying simulators, to applaud the ship's captain. She has made flying a passenger jet into a smooth art, as if a beautiful swan was coming into a flawless and graceful landing.*

*It seems appropriate to quote some of those comments below:*

*-This is just amazing how much skill, experience and pure intuition it must take! By far from any aerial manoeuvres including low altitude loops, carrier landings this is on par or above given the responsibility involved in delivering hundreds of passengers safely to a destination. Standing ovations!*

-Straightening and levelling the plane until a second before touch down. Kudos to both of them

-Seems like a walk in the park for them…on a Sunday afternoon….drinking a water bottle while on approach!  Lets see if Mr Bean can do it too!

-Look at how relax she is while doing the job… just-another-day-at-the-office like stuff.  Simply superb.

-That's awesome! Hopefully now I can get a higher score in the simulator. This one is really hard. I keep banging the plane into the ground right after I clear the mountain to reduce altitude. Looks like she kept further left and kept banking. Seems scary even in VR. I can't imagine that in real life

-This is the best I've seen on the internet thus far. I can watch this over and over and over and over. I totally enjoyed that approach and landing she hand flew it like a boss

-Wow!  For a minute there I thought I was watching Top Gun Maverick.  Awesome job! Watched it over and over.

-That is a former military pilot at the controls, textbook manoeuvres; no doubt about it.  I had to hold my breath the last few turns.

-Man, she is flying it like it is a Cessna. Big respect.


Seems a worthy comparison.


-Wow.  Whatever they're paying her….they should double it!

-Wooowwwww! That was pure joy. Despite the age of equality, it shouldn't and doesn't matter the Captain was a woman but I cannot lie the sight of that tiny lady almost weighed down by the four fat gold stripes on her shoulder boards, operating the controls in a focused yet effortless and graceful way - and seeing the aircraft swoosh and bank at her behest - added an extra special blend of spice and piquancy to an already incredible clip!!! My thanks to the people that brought us this marvellous sequence and of course to the Captain and her copilot….

-God bless the Commander and officer crew member in Jesus name, Amen

*-Captain must be an angel from heaven, working for God*

*-Amen Praise the Lord in Jesus Name Amen*

*Quite a few praised the Lord and prayed for the Captain, probably overlooking the tiny Buddha image stuck in the middle of the instrument panel.*

*-That was some seriously amazing flying. I want to marry that lady*

*Sorry, Captain Ugyen is married… to an Airbus 320neo (age of both is a secret).*

*-Great job – I have better wipers on my 1972 Mini!*

*-You'd think in these multi million dollar aircraft they could have better windshield wipers.*

*-Where did they get the windscreen wipers from! Off a series 1 Land Rover*

*Several viewers commented on the obsolete-looking windshield wipers on this Airbus320neo aircraft, as opposed to the very hi-tech dashboard panel.*

*-I'd definitely have to be diapered up for that approach.*

*-I wonder if she did her flight training in New Zealand?*

*Indeed, Captain Ugyen went to flight school in New Zealand, at Christchurch in January 2005.*

*-Oh God, Female Captain fiddling with knobs, hands on dashi! Scary…*

*-And my wife couldn't park her car without crashing it into the pole*

A few viewers took sniping sexist remarks regarding a female at the control of an airplane. My advice to them is that if they should fall ill, make sure to tell their male doctor not to use any X-ray on them, as it was invented by a woman, Madam Curie, who is the only person who has ever won two Nobel Prizes in two different fields of science.

I have always said doing anything well is a science, doing it extremely well is an art. It is perhaps most appropriate to end with Captain Ugyen's own words:

"I really do believe flying is an art. It is amazing to be able to strike the perfect balance of safety and comfort, making flying a jet into Paro feel easy and comfortable for the passengers. While humans were never meant to fly, with training, experience and persistence, we can develop an instinct that allows you to feel and fly even an Airbus like it's an extension of yourself into a place like Paro. Flying into the heart of the Himalayas is half the challenge...the prevailing and prominent weather conditions makes it the real challenge."

Landed Paro / 降落帕羅機場

She has indeed turned a science into an art.

FILM ON YOUTUBE:
https://www.youtube.com/watch?v=JFuZfKZWmk0

不丹女飛官

進入不丹空域的這段起降飛行，總是令人大驚失色，尤其對膽子比較小的人，動輒嚇得得斂聲屏氣，那也是常態。大概只有喜歡大玩雲霄飛車的孩子，才會享受這種驚心動魄的刺激感。

如果你覺得降落香港啟德舊機場的最後一個九十度轉彎已經算是高難度的降落，那麼，你不妨試試拉丁「八字形」的降落方式，或更準確地說，是「心煩意亂的多個八字形組合降落模式」，彷彿需要不斷妥協退讓再拐彎抹角似的，為難一台大客機繞著一座座山峰峽谷，兜兜轉轉後才能降落不丹的帕羅 (Paro) 機場。雖然帕羅機場名列全球最難降落的三大機場之一，但其實另外兩個機場只適合小型定翼機或短程垂直起降的螺旋槳飛機，而帕羅則是扎扎實實給標準的大型客機降落的機場。

八字飛行不只是個數字比喻，而是經常出現在無人機的飛行訓練模式中，或花式溜冰中騰空飛躍的訓練項目裡，但卻不是用在真正大客機的飛行降落，除非你開的是戰鬥機，而且在進行空中混戰。可以想見，其危險程度，非同小可，而且很真實。二〇〇四年，已逝友人鄧永鏘 (David Tang) 和一群朋友乘坐私人飛機飛往不丹共度他的五十歲生日。飛機降落過程中，機翼觸地後，飛機才完成降落，有驚也有險。住在紐約的好朋友朱蒂 (Judith) 把原本計畫好的不丹之旅取消，原因是她發現自己的私人飛機機長必須先在印度接受額外的飛行培訓才能獲准飛往不丹的帕羅機場。

說了這許多前提與故事，你或許可以理解我是帶著什麼樣的預設立場與先入為主的想法，來和尤茜 (Ugyen) 機長相約不丹首都廷布，面對面好好聊聊。當然，在此之前，我已來過這個美若仙境的國度好幾次，也曾應最資深的皇室成員——不丹皇太后的接待與邀請，在此執行過一些小型計畫案。

尤茜機長在我眼前出現時，身穿全套軍裝、頭戴帽子，外套肩上繡了四道槓，標準的機長制服。尤茜機長是不丹皇家航空 (Druk Air) 首位女機長；曾經一度，這是喜馬拉雅國度裡唯一一家敢於為此危險航線提供服務的航空公司，僅此一家，別無分店——降落要求務必精準，挑戰你的膽大心細。

不過，尤茜機長看起來並沒有想像中一副膽識過人的勇猛外型，事實上，也沒有那種雄赳赳、氣昂昂的男性氣慨。有關尤茜機長的故事，要從二十年前開始說起。二○○三年，尤茜高中畢業，聽說不丹皇家航空正在招聘飛行員。她心生好奇，決定把握時機，試試看。但航空公司當時只提供兩個名額的獎學金——一個全額、一個半額——而且只給男性，錄取者將受派到國外接受飛行訓練。看似時不我予，但尤茜在隔年認識了不丹籍的楚迪亞 (Chodea) 機長後，楚迪亞鼓勵她繼續追求飛行工作的目標。於是，尤茜把加

Flying into Paro Bhutan / 飛進不丹帕羅機場
Landing approach / 開始降落

Captain Ugyen in cockpit during flight /
機長尤茜飛行時在駕駛艙

入了不丹皇家航空作為志向，楚迪亞機長也成為她的其中一個教練。

尤茜最終成功說服家人，支持她去上飛行學院，因為課程所費不貲。二〇〇五年一月，尤茜遠赴國外，開始接受飛行訓練。班上二十多名受訓人員中，只有三、四名女學生。完成一年八個月的培訓課程後，尤茜獲得商用飛行機師證照，最後也達成最低飛行時數的條件。

二〇〇七年，她加入不丹皇家航空，開始飛行線訓練，一年多以後，尤茜在二〇〇九年五月正式成為副機師。她至今已飛了超過十年，累積飛行時數為七千個小時，並在二〇一八年正式被提升為機長。一直到二〇二二年的今天，尤茜的飛行紀錄已逾八千小時。今天，即使是資深飛行員也只有五十幾歲，資淺的飛行員獲晉升的機會少之又少。不過，如果就性別差異來說，和她剛加入時的「七個機長僅她一位女性」的比例來看，確實已有顯著變化——現在全體飛行員陣容中，已有四名女性。

不過，相對於其他國家的航空業，這樣的性別比例依舊低得多。尤茜告訴我，鄰國印度的女性飛行員不少，因為飛行過程中經常可以聽到無線對話中傳來女性的聲音。性別歧視者或許會駁斥，那是因為女性比較愛說話。但事實不然，印度的女性飛行員占總體飛行員超過百分之十二，已逾全球平均值的兩倍之多。

一如文章引言所述，飛入不丹境內是「非一般」的降落。由於不丹境內的特殊地勢與 C 類型跑道，不丹機場絕對嚴禁任何夜間降落，每一台降落帕羅機場的飛機，都必須遵守目視飛行規則。一般機場跑道的標準寬度是四十五公尺，但不丹的帕羅機場跑道只有三十公尺之寬。尤茜機長所駕駛的空巴 A320-neo 系列的最大載客量是一百四十人，機翼寬度超過三十五公尺，遠遠超過跑道寬度。至於 2265 公尺的跑道長度，也只能勉強足夠讓飛機起飛。除了跑道「不夠寬敞、餘裕有限」以外，機場還位於海拔 2244 公尺的高度上，與平地相比，高海拔較為稀薄的空氣也限制了飛機的升力。

Bangkok night approach / 曼谷夜晚接近

儘管如此，波音公司還是在帕羅機場剛把跑道建好後，立即派了一台 737-700 到不丹來完成十一次試飛。不過，不丹皇家航空最終還是捨波音而選購空巴的 A319 與 320 系列飛機。即使有中國等其他國家的巨額採購訂單，但這樣的趨勢或許並非特殊案例，在可預期的未來，可能演變成常態趨勢。烏克蘭戰爭已充分說明，美國出手的制裁行動，不分國界。有潛力的買家可能對波音公司所釋出的採購合約有所疑慮，因為誰也說不準，萬一政府因外在局勢或內部爭權的需要而一夜間反目成仇或失控無理時，買家就得承擔零件短缺或飛機維修的風險。

過去兩年，在全球疫情最高峰期間，尤茜機長為了醫療救援與物流補給而完成好幾趟飛行，包括緊急運送物資，其中也在印度的醫療體系不堪重負時，幾度將狀況危急的

Covid relief flight to Paro / Covid 物資抵達帕羅機場

不丹病患者從印度載送回本國接受治療。我們「中國探險學會」的一位董事也私下購買與提供相關的醫療設備，並空運到不丹。或許，尤茜機長也曾在過去的某趟飛行中，載送過這些物資。

在那段疲於奔命的過程中，每完成一趟飛行旅程後，尤茜都必須接受隔離，最初的二〇二〇年，隔離期間多達二十一天，後期疫情紓緩，隔離期限減為十四天。她體驗過兩次二十一天的隔離生活；而過去兩年內，尤茜其實已數不清到底自己度過了幾次十四天隔離的日子，直到今年年初，隔離天數才降為七天。她能在如此艱鉅的大環境下堅持對這份工作的投入與付出，已值得在她制服的肩膀上，再加槓嘉獎——沒有一道也值得加半道槓吧？

YouTube 上至少有兩部尤茜機長駕駛空巴客機降落帕羅機場的影片，我想更準確地說是，尤茜機長游刃有餘地操縱一台飛機的身影。其中拍得最好的一部是今年六月才上載線上的七分鐘版本，至今為止，已累積超過 170 萬人瀏覽，而且留言近千，好評如潮。她對這隻巨鳥飛機掌控自如的優雅與輕鬆駕馭的熟練，令許多同為飛行員者大為驚艷，也讓那些仍在練習使用模擬器學飛行的仰慕者，欽佩不已，忍不住要為這位機長拍手叫絕。尤茜把駕駛飛機當成流暢的藝術志業，仿若一隻美麗的天鵝，一個轉身便完成了無懈可擊的優雅降落。

A320n at Paro / 空巴 A320n 在帕羅機場

Everest on right taken by Captain Ugyen /
喜馬拉雅山於右側,機長尤茜拍攝

容我列舉一些人對尤茜機長的評論與留言:

～ 實在令人驚艷。這背後需要累積多少技巧、經驗和敏銳的直覺判斷啊!到目前為止,包括低空迴旋在內的所有空中動作,以及機身著陸等,都和數百名乘客是否能安全抵達目的地的重責大任緊密關聯。為她起立鼓掌!

～ 一直到飛機著陸前一秒才把機身拉直、拉平。為機長的這兩個動作喝采!

～ 看他們操控飛機,就像週日午後的公園散步……那麼悠然自在……抵達前還能從容不迫喝瓶水啊!我來看看豆豆先生是不是也能如法炮製。

～ 你看看她在工作時是多麼輕鬆嫻熟……好像「不過就是另一個稀鬆尋常的上班日」那種不慌不忙。超讚!

～ 太了不起了!真希望我能順利在飛行模擬器上得高分。這真的很難!每一次當我飛越山頂後降低高度,就不斷自撞地面。看起來她似乎不斷往左飛,而且還不斷傾斜機體。即使只用「虛擬實境」來看,也夠怵目驚心的了!我實在無法想像真正飛行的實況。

～這是我至今為止在網路上看過最完美的飛行視頻。我可以反覆不斷地看，真的百看不厭。我太喜歡看她飛行降落的方法，像個經驗老道的高手，駕馭自如。

～哇！有那麼一瞬間我以為《捍衛戰士：獨行俠》在我眼前上演。太厲害了！我看了一遍又一遍！

～這種飛行水準，簡直是前軍機飛手在掌控的飛行，真的不用懷疑，那是教科書裡才看得到的完美操作啊！最後幾個回合的拐彎轉身，看得我屏氣凝神，大氣不敢吸一口。

～天啊，她好像在飛一台「西斯納」的小型飛機！肅然起敬啊！

這是值得關注的相提並論！

～哇！不管她的薪資多少……她的公司都應該幫她雙倍加薪！

～嗚哇！置身其中就是純然享樂！雖然現在是男女平等的時代，機長是不是女性不重要，但眼前這幕我就不得不說幾句真話了——這位個子嬌小的女人幾乎被她制服肩膀上那四條粗壯的金色條槓壓得很沈重，但她卻能全神貫注又毫不費力，以優雅的姿勢來掌控所有裝置配備——你只會看著飛機在她的掌控與指揮下，呼嘯來去——她超高技藝，把這段本來就已經酷到難以置信的飛行片段加辣加料！！！非常感謝給我們錄製這段精彩視頻的人，當然還要感謝機長和她的副駕駛……。

～懇求上帝保祐機長和機組成員，奉耶穌的名，阿門。
～這位機長一定是來自天堂的天使，下落凡間為上帝工作。

～阿門！奉主耶穌的名感謝讚美主！阿門！

留言中還不少人為此感謝讚美上帝，同時為機長祈禱；看來大家都輕忽了插在儀表板上的小佛像喔。

～ 那真的是無比驚人的飛行啊！怎麼辦，好想和這位女士結婚喔！

抱歉喔，尤茜機長嫁人了……嫁給空巴 320neo( 別問，雙方年齡都是秘密 )。

～ 幹得好啊！只是……只是飛機的雨刷……我覺得家裡那台 1972 年 Mini 小車雨刷，比飛機的雨刷更好欸！
～你可能會以為這台數千萬美元的飛機應該配上更好的雨刷才對，但……事實不然。
～飛機上的雨刷哪裡來的啊？！不會是六十年代路虎車的系列雨刷吧！

好幾位留言者對這台空巴 320neo 上早該淘汰的破雨刷很有意見，但卻對一整面高科技的儀表面板讚譽有加。

Into the clouds / 飛進雲裡

Drukair wings / 不丹皇家航空機翼

～ 操作這種驚險萬分的降落，我肯定要包尿布了。
～ 我好奇她是不是在紐西蘭完成飛行訓練啊？

沒錯，尤茜機長確實在二〇〇五年一月時到紐西蘭接受她的飛行訓練。

～ 天啊，女機長出手，親自上陣！驚艷指數爆表啊……。
～ 和我老婆差太多了，她如果沒撞到柱子是停不了車的……。

其中有些看過視頻的觀眾對「女性操控飛機實情」發表了充滿性別歧視的言論。我對這些人的建議是，有一天如果他們病倒了，一定要告訴他們的男性醫師，萬萬不可讓他們接受 X 光檢查，因為那是由女科學家居禮夫人發明的東西，而這位偉大的科學家，是至今唯一一位曾在兩個不同的科學領域獲頒諾貝爾獎的人。

我常說，把一件事做好，那是科學；把一件事做得極致，那是藝術。或許尤茜機長自己說過的一番話，就是最貼切的結論：

「我確實相信，飛行是藝術。能夠兼顧安全與舒適，追求兩者之間的平衡，好讓我的乘客在飛往帕洛機場的飛機上感到輕鬆愜意，那是很奇特又美好的經驗。人類雖然飛不了，但透過訓練與經驗的累積，以及堅持不懈的努力，我們得以發展出這種近乎本能的專業，使你接近一種飛行的感覺，你甚至可以把空中巴士當成你身體的部分延伸；悠然駕馭一架飛行器，進入像帕羅這樣的地方。飛越喜馬拉雅山的中心區域，只算完成一半的挑戰……另一半真正的挑戰是它異於尋常與特殊難料的天候條件。」

尤茜確實把獨門科學轉化為一場藝術。

*Youtube* 上的相關影片：*https://www.youtube.com/watch?v=JFuZfKZWmk0*

Landed Bangkok safely / 安全降落曼谷

依
揚
想
亮 出版書目

國家圖書館出版品預行編目 (CIP) 資料

齊物逍遙 . 2023 = Enlightened sojourn/ 黃效文著 . -- 初版 . --
新北市 : 依揚想亮人文事業有限公司 , 2023.11
面 ; 公分
中英對照
ISBN 978-626-96174-4-9( 平裝 )
1.CST: 遊記 2.CST: 世界地理
719                                                                112014179

齊
物
逍
遙 2023

作者‧黃效文｜攝影‧黃效文｜發行人‧劉鋆｜美術編輯‧Rene、鍾京燕｜責任編輯‧王思晴｜翻譯‧
童貴珊｜法律顧問‧達文西個資暨高科技法律事務所｜出版社‧依揚想亮人文事業有限公司｜經銷商‧
聯合發行股份有限公司｜地址‧新北市新店區寶橋路 235 巷 6 弄 6 號 2 樓｜電話‧02 2917 8022｜印刷‧
禹利電子分色有限公司｜初版一刷‧2023 年 11 月（平裝）｜定價 1500 元｜ISBN‧978-626-96174-4-9｜